IN CHRIST ALL THINGS HOLD TOGETHER

Jock Stein served the Presbyterian Church of East Africa for three years and is now minister of The Steeple Church, Dundee. He is a member of the Church of Scotland Panel on Doctrine, a former member of the Scottish Scripture Union Council, and chairman of Street Level Festival.

He is the editor of *Ministers for the 1980s*, published in 1979 by The Handsel Press.

Howard Taylor spent ten years in Malawi, working as a parish minister and teaching at a theological college for the Church of Central Africa (Presbyterian). He is now minister of three parish churches in Argyll. He wrote the 1982–3 prayer guide for members of the Church of Scotland, and has also written a catechism for the Christian Literature Association in Malawi.

Christ is the image of the invisible God, the first-born of all creation ... he is before all things, and in him all things hold together. He is the head of his body, the church; he is the beginning, the first-born from the dead, that in everything he might have the first place.

(Colossians 1:15,17–18)

Howard Taylor
Jock Stein

IN CHRIST
ALL THINGS
HOLD TOGETHER

An Introduction to
Christian Doctrine

WIPF & STOCK · Eugene, Oregon

Wipf and Stock Publishers
199 W 8th Ave, Suite 3
Eugene, OR 97401

In Christ All Things Hold Together
An Introduction to Christian Doctrine
By Stein, Jock and Taylor, Howard
Copyright© The Handsel Press
ISBN 13: 978-1-57910-444-3
Publication date 3/9/2010
Previously published by The Handsel Press, 1984

Contents

Preface

JS: How did all this begin, Howard?

HGT: In 1976 my work as a parish minister for the Church of Central Africa (Presbyterian) was interrupted for about eighteen months. I was asked to teach Systematic Theology and the History of Doctrine at one of the Church's Theological Colleges. I learned a lot of theology in the process! And I came to appreciate all the more what we learned at New College, Edinburgh in the late 1960s.

JS: Isn't it just as important to be training elders, youth leaders and church members?

HGT: You're biased, because that's what you did in Kenya! Actually I had many opportunities in Malawi to speak to all kinds of groups. I was always impressed by their sincerity, but disturbed by the number of folk who would say that Christ died for their sins, yet had little idea what it meant. This was true of Europeans as well as Africans.

JS: Did anyone ever ask you to write a book?

HGT: In Easter 1978 the interdenominational 'New Life for All' organization asked me to give a series of talks on the meaning of the death and resurrection of Christ. When the meetings were over, I was asked to put down in writing what I had said.

JS: But talks and lectures are often a bit dry in book form.

HGT: That's where you come in, Jock. You can have a free hand to rewrite the book and fill in any gaps.

JS: Do you think that people in Scotland, and other Western countries, have much to gain from teaching coming originally from Africa?

HGT: I believe the West has more to learn from Africa than

the other way round! But this is a book on Christian doctrine – not about worship, or Christian ethics, or church order, where the local situation has a bigger influence. Let's pray that God may use it to help Christians in more than one continent.

Introduction

This is the age of the market. Books have to be written and packaged for particular people in particular places. 'Is this book academic or popular?' 'Is it published for people in Malawi or Scotland or anywhere?' 'Is it for enquirers or mature Christians?'

And yet we are *all* commanded to love God with our mind and strength. The Bible is for *all*, not just the experts. Writers like C. S. Lewis and William Barclay managed to bridge the gap between popular and academic. It can be done. There was a time in Scotland when a manual worker could discuss theology with a professor. He had learned to think in ideas as well as pictures, in concepts as well as stories.

This still happens today, especially when both share a common faith in one Lord Jesus Christ. Theology is that kind of subject. It is a dialogue between the mind of man and the mind of God, possible through Jesus Christ who is both man and God.

This particular book assumes that Christian faith is true: that God really is God, that he cares for the world, that Jesus Christ is the eternal Son of God who was born to share our weak humanity and who rose again from death. All that and much more. It is said, even by some who should know better, that modern man can no longer understand these things, for he inhabits a different kind of world; it is said that truth is no more than 'truth-for-you' or 'truth-for-me'. Christian faith, on the contrary, starts with Jesus Christ who said 'I am the way, the truth and the life' (John 14:6). In saying 'I am', he links his own being with that of God, the first and the last, who is, and was, and is to come (Revelation 1:8). Truth is therefore for all — we are not isolated individuals, encapsulated by our own twentieth-century outlook, but men and women who share a common humanity with people of every age and culture (Acts 17:25–28).

Is this starting point, are these assumptions an irrational leap of faith? Not at all. God reveals himself in such a way that his revelation can be received by man, and the content of this revelation is the Gospel of Jesus Christ. To receive this revelation is the reasonable thing to do, because Jesus himself is God's 'reason', or Word (John 1:1–18). It is the unreasonable man who refuses to listen to the Word from God.

This book has four sections. You can start with any section and read it as a whole, although they follow on. Part One is about how we know God, and will be of special interest to those who know a bit of philosophy and a bit of science. Part Two looks at man in the universe, and how Christian theology gives us a 'handle' on our human situation. Part Three looks more directly at Jesus Christ, who brings man and God together; and Part Four examines the life of faith in the fellowship of God's people.

Such an approach is sometimes called 'systematic theology'. This phrase can easily be misunderstood. True systematic theology is not an attempt to put all the pieces of Christian belief together in a closed, self-explanatory system, like a person making a picture out of a jigsaw puzzle. The truth of God is not contained within a system! It is Christ who is the Truth. The purpose of theological writing is to point to the truth which (or who!) is beyond it.

Christian theology is not a closed system incapable of being further enlightened or reformed by the light of God in Christ. This book simply attempts an orderly exposition of Christian beliefs. We hope that four kinds of people in particular will benefit from reading it:

The enquirer who wants to discover how Christian faith fits together, and how it sheds light on human life.

The committed Christian who is familiar with the Bible but has not yet managed to see Christian faith as a whole.

Introduction

The thoughtful person who is unable to reconcile the particular emphases of some sections of the Church with the Bible and Christian common sense.

The first-year divinity student who is looking for a perspective to theology in the tradition of the early Fathers and the Reformers.

NOTES

1. The writers assume that those who read this book will also be reading the Bible. To save space, only a few references are given in the text, although the Bible is often quoted or paraphrased.
2. Where Bible references are given, they are not from any one single version, although the language usually reflects the Revised Standard Version, often the Good News Bible, and occasionally the New International Version.
3. The words 'man' and 'men', 'he' and 'him', are normally used to include both sexes.
4. Parts One, Two, Three and Four can be read separately, or in sequence.
5. Each chapter ends with some suggestions for further reading, from a variety of viewpoints. Books marked * are more difficult.

PART ONE

Knowing God

CHAPTER ONE

Science and Faith

To be wise is to know God, ourselves and the world of nature

Calvin began his famous *Institutes of the Christian Religion* by saying that true wisdom consists almost entirely of two parts: the knowledge of God, and the knowledge of ourselves; and that these two parts of knowledge are bound together because only through knowing God do we come to know ourselves.

What Calvin says is very true. We are created and redeemed by God for a purpose. It follows that if we really want to know where we came from, who we are and where we are going, we must also know God and his purpose for us in creation and redemption.

But we must go further. Knowledge of the natural world is also part of true wisdom; for not only did God create and redeem man, he created the world in which we live, and his redemption of man will affect nature also. The whole creation waits eagerly for God to reveal his sons, Paul tells us in Romans chapter 8. God created man in nature, and gave him authority over nature. It follows that true wisdom consists not only of the knowledge of God and of ourselves, but also of our God-given relationship to the natural world.

Nature points beyond itself but cannot lead us to know God directly. Natural science and theology each have their appropriate ways of knowing

Can we come to know God by looking at, and examining what he has created? Can NATURE lead us directly to some kind of knowledge of God? Many in the past believed that it could. They believed a 'natural knowledge' of God was possible and indeed necessary. The subject they built round it was called 'natural theology'. Thomas Aquinas taught five ways one could (he thought) prove the existence of God by observing the world of nature. These ways are fully discussed and usually shown to be inconclusive in almost any modern book dealing with the philosophy of religion. The so-called argument from design is one that appeals to many. When we look at the wonderful balance of nature, the fantastic construction of every living thing, does this not prove that there is a good and infinite Designer behind it all? Well it certainly does not prove that the Designer is infinite, although it may be argued that he is powerful. It does not necessarily prove the goodness of the Designer, because there is much evil and suffering in the world. Now Christians know that this evil came not from the Designer. But we do not know this from nature; we know it from the self-revelation of God in Christ, which we receive in faith.

But the most fundamental objection to natural theology is that the examination and study of nature can only lead us to a greater knowledge of nature. It can tell us nothing about what is beyond nature. But the study of nature (whether as a casual observer or as a professional scientist) should lead us to see that nature is not self-explanatory, and therefore we are without excuse if we refuse to seek to know what is beyond nature (Romans 1:20).

What we do find when we examine the universe is that it is a natural phenomenon following regular patterns. The atheist or agnostic then go on to assume that there is no need to add God to the total picture; they say the universe is in principle self-explanatory. But that does not follow.

The Christian belief is that beyond nature there is One who created nature out of nothing and gave it its rational structure. The task of natural science is to explore this. In the very nature of the case, science cannot reach what is beyond nature.

It follows from this that natural science cannot explain

16

how nature came into existence, because that belongs to another level of enquiry. Thus, however far natural science advances, we shall still be left with questions about the origin, or genesis, of nature, and about the basis of nature's rational structure. This is explained further in chapter 6.

Natural science does not and should not operate with God as part of its data, but what it discovers points beyond nature to the glory of God. This not only applies to astrophysics and the study of minute particles of matter, but also to the wonder of nature which we see all the time in our daily lives.

The subject matter of theology is first and foremost the knowledge of God, because it is from knowing God that knowledge of ourselves and our place in nature comes. As our knowledge of God unfolds, we also learn about ourselves and our place in the world.

The way of knowing any object is determined by the object we wish to know. If we want to learn about a star we must use a telescope; to examine a tiny insect we would need a microscope; if we tried to use a telescope for the insect we would get nowhere. The way of knowing God is faith.

We know God by faith – not a special aptitude but reliance on God through his Word. To demand proof of God prior to trusting him is unscientific

FAITH is being sure of what we hope for, having certain knowledge of what we do not see (Hebrews 11:1). Faith is not a sixth (or seventh) sense – it is not a particular kind of emotion. In faith we humbly entrust ourselves to God, and learn to understand and to do what he says. When God says in Hebrew idiom, 'My son, give me your heart', this means in modern English, 'Give me your love in learning to know me and obey me'. Although knowledge of God may indeed affect our senses, we do not use our senses to come to know God. However, God does use analogies from our senses, especially the sense of hearing, since God reveals himself primarily to us

17

by his Word, and a word is heard, not seen. We are also expected to see what God does in history, and in the lives of people – but without God's Word and Spirit we fail to understand it (Isaiah 6:9).

It is because faith is knowledge of the unseen God that we walk by faith and not by sight, as Paul says. The word faith, however, has been devalued by over-use, so that its meaning often seems vague. It is far from vague in its effect. Just because it is knowledge of God, and therefore also knowledge of ourselves, it affects us in our deepest being. In faith we are challenged to our roots; our mind and spirit are renewed in repentance towards God and our fellow men.

Faith, belief and trust are three English words coming from one biblical root. So fundamental is faith to Christianity that Christians are called 'believers'. Faith is committal of one's entire self to God and his Gospel.

Faith is not an inspired guess. It is not an irrational leap into the dark. Faith is response to revelation, that is, to God's Word. It is brought to birth in us by the Holy Spirit when we hear the Word of God. It is not as though we must have faith in order to hear God's Word, rather, faith comes from hearing that Word.

Faith then is the way of knowing God. If an astronomer found a previously unknown star through his telescope, he might well invite his fellow astronomers to look through his telescope to see the star, or check his research for themselves. If they refused to come until he had demonstrated the existence of the star in some other way, we would regard their refusal as irrational, since the only way of knowing the star is through the instruments of astronomy. There can be no prior (*a priori*) proof of the star's existence.

Similarly when men refuse to open their hearts in faith to God, but demand prior proof of his existence outside of the context of faith, they are being unreasonable and indeed unscientific.

To take the illustration a little further, it sometimes happens that an astronomer says, 'I think there must be a new star somewhere in that area', because of some theory he has begun to hold, and then he tests out the theory by looking for the star. (This was in fact how the planet Pluto was discovered.) But until the discovery is actually made, scientists will always quarrel over the theory. So with the existence of God; there are good reasons why we should search for him; but until we find him by faith we can never reach agreement about him, and some will even doubt his existence.

We have said that knowledge of God affects us in our deepest being. Actually any truly scientific enquiry affects the enquirer himself. The astronomer must allow what the star tells him through his telescope to change his previous convictions. His openness to the star must involve the willingness to be changed or to 'repent'. Thus the true scientist, whether he be an astronomer or a theologian, is not a detached observer; on the contrary he must be committed as a person to his work.

This is why studying the Bible in so-called 'scientific detached objectivity' is often just a refusal to repent, and does not lead to a true knowledge of what the Bible is about. Such detachment is not scientific in the least. We should never put 'faith' against 'science' as if faith was somehow unreasonable, or even something to be a little ashamed of! Faith is not the starting point, the bottom rung of a ladder we build to reach up to God. It is the proper human way we find and use the ladder God himself has provided through his Word.

SUGGESTIONS FOR FURTHER READING

In the Bible   Proverbs 1, Psalm 111, 1 Peter 1

A Book   *Dogmatics in Outline,* by Karl Barth (chaps. 1–4) (SCM)
The Dissuaders, by D. W. D. Shaw (SCM)
Belief in Science and in Christian Life, Ed. T. F. Torrance (esp. chap. 1) (Handsel Press)

CHAPTER TWO

Where we Begin

Knowing God involves dialogue and reconciliation

A star is a thing, and God is a Person (or personal Being, if you prefer – the word 'person' might suggest only a clever guy somewhere up in the sky!). Our own involvement in the knowledge of any person, and especially God, is greater than in our knowledge of a thing. We get to know a person by listening to him speaking to us and we must respond. In knowing another there must be DIALOGUE. Only in this way can we enter into a personal relationship with the one we wish to know. Furthermore, in order to have this personal relationship we must allow the dialogue to bring us into a relationship of peace with him. We cannot get to know a person we hate, or with whom there is mutual distrust. There must be RECONCILIATION too.

So it is in our knowledge of God. We know him by opening the ears of our inmost being and listening to him. 'He who has ears to hear, let him hear', Jesus said. God takes the initiative in the dialogue; his Word is spoken. Changing the metaphor, we can say that his hand is knocking, his light has begun to shine. 'The light of the glory of God is revealed in the face of Jesus Christ' (2 Corinthians 4:6). 'This is the judgement, that light has come into the world and men have loved darkness rather than light' (John 3:19).

The response to his Word is faith, and in faith we begin to know him. His Word speaks to us not only about himself but about ourselves, challenging us and calling in question our whole way of life. His Word tells us that we need to be reconciled to him, for without that we cannot know him. The power of reconciliation is in that Word. Eternal life is knowledge of God and his Son (John 17:3).

Thus the way of knowing God is painful. It involves a 'crucifixion' of ourselves. We would be surprised if those friends of the astronomer we mentioned in chapter 1 really refused to come and look through the telescope to find for themselves the star they had been told about. Should we be surprised if men refuse to open their hearts in faith to God and his Gospel, and are left to flounder in the blindness (or deafness) of atheism and agnosticism? Yet the crucifixion of ourselves which comes through faith is not a destruction of ourselves, least of all our minds. With any genuine crucifixion there comes resurrection. We are not destroyed but renewed. 'Be transformed by the renewal of your minds', Paul says (Romans 12:2).

Faith is our response to God's Word of Truth, who is Jesus Christ

THE WORD. What then is God's Word to us? The writer to the Hebrews tells us that 'in many and various ways God spoke of old to our fathers by the prophets; but in these last days he has spoken to us by a Son' (Hebrews 1:1–2). John in his gospel describes this Son as the eternal Word of God, who has 'become a human being and lived among us' (John 1:14). Just as we express ourselves in words, so God has expressed himself to us in the person of his Son who is called 'the Word'. In the conception and birth of the Son of God into our human life (his incarnation), the Word of God has taken visible shape in the world.

Christ as the Word of God reveals God himself to us. There is no unknown God behind the back of Jesus whom we need fear. 'He who has seen me has seen the Father', Jesus said. In Christ God has stooped to our level and spoken to us in a language we can understand, just as an earthly father deals with his own child. The character of God is completely revealed to us on the cross, in his self-giving love. At the cross we also see ourselves judged because of our sin. 'Now is the judgement of this world', Jesus said, speaking of his death. Further, in the whole righteous life of Jesus on earth, we see our true human life revealed; we see humanity as God intended when he made man in his own image. And in the resurrection of Jesus we see the future that God intends for our human nature.

Thus the knowledge of God and of ourselves are brought together in the incarnation, life, death and resurrection of Jesus Christ, Son of God and son of man. He is the Word of God to us – the Word of Truth. He is the truth (John 14:6).

Christ speaks to us by the Holy Spirit, who awakens faith within us

THE SPIRIT. Christ is God's Word to us. But how do we grasp that Word when Christ is no longer physically here? We cannot literally see him with our eyes, or hear him with our ears. His bodily presence has been withdrawn from us. How then can we know him? Just by reading a book about him (the Bible), or listening to what the Church says about him? The link from us to God through Christ is faith, we said above. How then does this faith grow within us? After Jesus left the world he gave the Holy Spirit to his disciples, so that through the worship and mission of his people, the world might hear God's Word and know him through Christ. The bond uniting man to Christ is faith, but prior to that, Christ comes to man through the Holy Spirit (who is also called the Spirit of Christ, the Spirit of Jesus and the Spirit of God).

How exactly does the Spirit work in us to draw us to Christ? We must be careful not to say too much. The Spirit shares God's freedom, like the wind which 'blows where it wills' (John 3:8). Our experience differs: theology is not the same as psychology: trying to define the Spirit's work from a study of the human mind is just as inappropriate as trying to know God through observing nature.

It is the Spirit who warms our hearts in love to God and

our fellow man. We are often exhorted in the New Testament to 'pray in the Spirit'. The Holy Spirit is the source of what we might call our CHRISTIAN EXPERIENCE.

The Holy Spirit also lives in the Church, or CHRISTIAN COMMUNITY. It is in the Spirit that the community is called into existence, and from the Spirit that it gets its life. The Church's purpose is to lead men to bear witness to Christ as Lord, and to worship him as God's Son. By Church we mean the Christian community which goes right back in history, in fellowship and in doctrine, to the apostles and even to the Old Testament prophets.

Even though our experience, and the community, are vital for our knowledge of God in Christ, they stand subordinate to the SCRIPTURES. Again it is the Holy Spirit who has inspired the Bible, but there are a number of things which make the Scriptures of Old and New Testaments the highest authority on earth that the Spirit uses to bring us to know God in the Gospel.

The Bible is prior in authority to the Church and Christian experience, but all three should lead us to Christ

THE BIBLE. Whereas the Church and our Christian experience are subject to change and error, the Bible does not change, even though we always have to translate the original writings into the languages of today.

Furthermore, the inspired writers and compilers of the Scriptures were either the witnesses or the interpreters of God's great redemptive acts: in Israel, in the birth and earthly life of Christ, in his resurrection and ascension, in the outpouring of the Holy Spirit on the day of Pentecost.

The gospels and the New Testament letters tell us in many places the purpose God had when he inspired and gave us the Scriptures: it was to lead us to salvation in Christ. We cannot begin to understand the Bible properly unless we grasp this. Also we cannot understand the Church or our Christian experience without realizing that their purpose too is to lead us into deeper union with Christ. So the Bible, the Church and our Christian experience belong inseparably together.

At this point, someone may ask, 'Yes, but which parts of the Bible? Do we still need the Old Testament, for example?'

In the second century AD, a man named Marcion dismissed the Old Testament as primitive and barbaric, of no use for an understanding of God. This view has been clearly rejected by mainstream Christianity down the ages. However, although most Christians would acknowledge that the Old Testament does have an important place in our knowledge of God, many find it difficult to say how. Our knowledge of God is *fully* apprehended in Jesus Christ, whom we do not meet in person until the New Testament – so how then can the Old Testament help us?

The purpose of Israel and the Old Testament

ISRAEL. God begins, from a distance as it were, to draw near to the world in Israel, and he comes into the world within Israel in the birth of Christ. God's drawing near to sinful men must mean judgement and forgiveness and this is what we find in Israel's history fulfilled on the cross. In the cross of Jesus the fullness of the revelation of God's character is given to us. Yet all that has gone before, in God's dealing with his people Israel, points forward to the final and full revelation. Only when God actually comes into the world do we see him clearly; but before that we do see him, even though 'as from afar'. This Old Testament view of God is not as clear as in the New, but it is none the less *real*. It is the God and Father of our Lord Jesus who is drawing near to his people. So in a real sense the saints of ancient Israel did see God, and what they saw foreshadowed the coming of Christ. 'Abraham rejoiced to see my day,' Jesus said, 'he saw it and was glad.'

In fact, one place where an atheist or agnostic could well begin is with the Jews. They have been called 'the one natural proof of God's existence'. What is the secret of this race who returned only this century to their homeland? What is the meaning of their call to be 'a light to the Gentiles'? Why should they have faced the horror of Auschwitz? Who is the mysterious figure in Isaiah chapter 53 who suffers on our behalf? Is it Christ, true son of Adam and son of Israel, to whom the mystery and suffering of Israel point?

The coming of the New Testament does not mean that the Old Testament can be done away with. On the contrary, it brings the Old Testament into focus and enables us to understand it more fully. Seen then through the lens of the New Testament the Old Testament gives us a beautiful picture of God.

When he revealed his glory to Moses, God revealed himself as 'The LORD, a God merciful and gracious, slow to anger and abounding in steadfast love and faithfulness, maintaining love for thousands of generations, forgiving wickedness, rebellion and sin; but who will not fail to punish the guilty . . .' (Exodus 34:6–7).

In this remarkable statement we have the forgiveness and mercy of God brought together with his righteous judgement. How can the two come from the one God? The answer is found in the New Testament statement that God is love, and fully revealed in the New Testament explanation of the meaning of the cross. We come back to this very important point later on.

In Egypt God revealed himself as a compassionate God who in his pity for his people saved them by his power. The Old Testament prophets spoke, however, not only of the everlasting mercy and kindness of God, but also of his anger, and so they often prophesied that God would, using his power, punish his people.

It is because God loves the world and its people that he is angry with anything that spoils the world or causes suffering to people. That is why the anger of God is real and his judgement something to be reckoned with.

From our belief that God is love, we can see that it follows that he is both a merciful God and a God who judges the sinner. He is 'the Holy One of Israel', a Righteous Judge of his creation. He is faithful and true. He is not arbitrary in character, but self-consistent and to be relied upon.

The glory and character of God are brought fully to focus in the face of Jesus Christ, who is the fulfilment of the Law and the prophets (Luke 24:44). In Christ we have revealed God's amazing love to sinful mankind, in that he himself suffers for us. He took our human flesh upon himself, lived the life of a poor man, and died a cruel death between two criminals. God's love for us is a self-giving love; he does not love us from a distance, but comes right to us, becoming bone of our bone and flesh of our flesh in his Son Jesus Christ. God shows his love to us in that while we were still sinners Christ died for us.

The anger of God too is revealed in the Gospel. Speaking of his coming death upon the cross, Jesus said 'Now is the judgement of this world'. The cross of Christ is God's sentence of death against man in his rebellion. The magnitude of the rebellion is seen in the fact that it led to the death of the Son of God. In accepting that judgement of God against us in the cross, we hear the other word from the cross, 'Father forgive'. And we are forgiven.

It is in the cross of Jesus that we most plainly see that God is love, for in the cross we see his mercy and his judgement brought together. So that we can say, from another angle, that the cross is where we begin.

SUGGESTIONS FOR FURTHER READING

In the Bible   Exodus 3, Psalm 51, Luke 24

A Book   *Creation and Redemption*, by George Florovsky
               (chap. 2) (Nordland, USA)
               Doctrine of the Knowledge of God, by T. H. L. Parker
               (Oliver & Boyd)
               Theological Science, by T. F. Torrance (Oxford
               University Press)

CHAPTER THREE

How to Understand the Bible

The Truth is Jesus Christ – not the Bible, the Church or Christian experience

It is not as though the TRUTH is found by adding what we find in the Bible to what we find in the Church and our Christian experience. The Church and our spiritual experience do not add to the Bible, but bring into focus our apprehension of Christ through Bible reading. The truth is in Christ, and Christ is not identical with the Bible or the Church or our experience. Failure to realize this can and so often does lead to the error of the Jews, to whom Jesus spoke when he said, 'You search the Scriptures for in them you think you have eternal life; they indeed bear witness to me, yet you refuse to come to me that you may have life' (John 5:39–40).

The Bible is like a window in an otherwise dark room, through which the light of truth shines. Through the glass we see reality beyond. If we want to understand the purpose of glass we must allow light to shine through it. The reality we wish to know is not in the window, but the window is necessary if we are to know it. This applies not only to the Bible but also the Church and our Christian experience.

Failure to apply the above principles of the knowledge of truth leads to all kinds of disagreements within the Church today. There are so many sects who claim loyalty to the Bible – so-called liberal or radical theologians, pietists, those who hold the view that the Church is the dispenser of truth, and many others who would make claims which distort the truth of the Gospel of Jesus Christ. It is also responsible for some of the dryness and deadness of Bible study and debate found in much that is called 'conservative evangelical' Christianity today.

29

The Bible is inspired by God to bring people to know him through Jesus Christ, the key to Scripture

There has been much dispute, especially in the last two centuries, about the INSPIRATION OF THE BIBLE. Very few indeed hold the view that the Bible writers were merely God's secretaries, although many have claimed that the inspiration is a verbal inspiration reaching the actual words written. In some parts a prophet or apostle is claiming to give a message direct from God; in other parts the writer has clearly given careful thought to the subject matter over a period of time; in yet other parts an editor has put together earlier writings (e.g. the Psalms).

In some circles the word 'infallible' is used, while others use 'trustworthy' to describe the Scriptures. In our view it is quite enough to say the Bible has been inspired by the Spirit and is a unique piece of writing given by God for the purpose of leading men to salvation in Christ. Many people quote 2 Timothy 3:16, which says that all Scripture is inspired by God, but forget the immediately preceding verse which says that the sacred writings are able to instruct for salvation through faith in Christ Jesus. It is this verse 15 which gives the purpose of inspiration. Thus it follows quite logically that the Bible must be interpreted by the Gospel of Christ to which through the Spirit it leads us.

The Bible points to Christ only in the context of Christian experience and the Church (or Community of God) which goes back in history to the apostles and prophets. The Bible cannot be interpreted by itself alone. You cannot interpret Scripture by Scripture alone in isolation from the workings of the Spirit. If you do try this you find it like a great jigsaw puzzle of verses which have to be fitted together. There are so many ways of fitting them together that Bible study becomes completely bewildering, if divorced from Christ. The number of sects each claiming to be Bible-based is evidence for this. Of course, it is impossible to fit them together into a complete picture, so men are forced to add their own thoughts and

30

traditions to complete the picture. This is what the Pharisees did!

Some use special principles of interpretation for understanding the Bible, for example, 'the Eternal Decrees of God', or 'Liberation'. These become the key to understanding the whole Bible; the results of these particular examples are usually in the first instance to limit Christ's atonement to the elect, and in the second to focus the Gospel narrowly on political change.

But the main error we are here talking about is to identify truth with the actual words of Scripture. It is Jesus who says to the Jews, 'Why do you not understand what I say [my words]?' 'It is because you cannot bear to hear my Word [*Logos*].' In order to understand the words of Scripture we have to hear the Logos, Christ himself. The words of Scripture lead us beyond themselves to the Eternal Word. When we allow the Bible so to lead us, then we recognize that although it has many human authors it is God who has given it to us.

The opposite error to the one we have been discussing is made by much of what is called 'modern theology'. This is to cut the words of Scripture off from reality so that they have no reference to objective truth in Christ at all. This is to divorce language from reality. In this kind of so-called theology, the purpose of the study of Scripture is not to come to know God; it is only to come to a self-understanding. According to this kind of Bible study, when, for example, the apostles spoke about the resurrection of Christ, they were really speaking about a self-understanding that Jesus by his life and death had helped them to come to. They were not talking about anything that happened to Jesus after his death. But this is to turn theology into some kind of anthropology or sociology – speaking about man, not about God.

Some of what is called 'scientific biblical scholarship' is in fact unscientific and irrational, although superficially it may have the appearance of being rational and objective. To illustrate this we will use the example of a telescope again. The

31

world's great telescopes are amazing instruments full of all kinds of gadgets to enable the astronomer to come to a knowledge of the particular part of the heavens he is viewing. Let us imagine a team of technicians coming to examine this instrument and make some sense of it, without realizing that its purpose is to view distant objects in the skies beyond it. They will all try to work out what this and that gadget is for, and write many learned papers about them. If they are writing independently of one another they will all have different ideas about which parts of the instrument are useful and which are useless, which were original and which were later additions, which are fundamental and which are merely superficial. What is certain is that they will never be able to make sense of it as a whole until they discover what it is for, and they won't discover that until they actually look through it. Once they have made this fundamental discovery then they will be able gradually to make sense of the whole. As they actually use the telescope for its purpose of viewing reality beyond it in the heavens then it will, as it were, be able to unfold its many and varied riches to them and they will see it as a wonderful unity. If they refuse to take into account the purpose of the telescope in their investigations we would have to say that the whole basis of their work is irrational even though it has the appearance of being scientific. This is why some of the 'assured results of modern biblical scholarship' can be so easily contradicted by the next generation of experts.

There will still be parts of the Bible we don't understand and even parts which seem to run counter to our knowledge of Christ, but we will not just reject these parts nor will we desperately try to explain them with all sorts of fantastic arguments. We will instead let the light of Christ shine through the whole. If there are parts of the telescope we don't understand then the best way to identify what is wrong (especially if it is the lenses that are causing the problem) is to let the light shine through so that the dark places are exposed. One kind of approach, sometimes criticized as 'fundamentalist', through clever juggling tries desperately to fit all these dark parts into a system; another kind of approach, sometimes criticized as 'liberal', just cuts them out. But the parts cut out always vary from age to age according to the prevailing philosophy of the day! The right approach is to seek to be governed by the one truth to which the Scriptures point.

How the Bible, Church and experience are related

Earlier we compared the Bible with a window in an otherwise dark room through which we see reality beyond. The reality is not in the glass, but the window is necessary if we are to see the reality beyond. We have also spoken of our Christian experience and the Church as instruments the Holy Spirit uses to bring us to God in Christ. Changing the illustration of the window slightly, we could compare the Bible, our Christian experience and the Church to three lenses in a telescope through which the light must shine if we are to see clearly the reality beyond. It seems to us that there are three basic mistakes in dealing with these lenses.

The first mistake comes from removing one lens altogether. The result is a blurred image indeed. For example, if we dispense with the necessity of the Christian experience of prayer, worship, and devotion and don't allow the Bible and the Church to have any effect on our day-to-day lives, then our religion is nothing but dead orthodoxy. If on the other hand we dispense with the teaching and discipline of the Church which goes back in history to the apostles and prophets, then we are in danger of fanaticism, spiritual pride and sectarianism.

The second mistake is to imagine that the truth is in one of the lenses instead of beyond it. This of course is quite absurd. It would be like removing a lens from the telescope and examining it as if that could bring knowledge of the reality of the star. This is equivalent with identifying truth with the Bible, the Church or our Christian experience.

We have already discussed how this error relates to the Bible. It is also found in those who identify truth with the Church. For example, one view is that a Church Council or the Church hierarchy is the dispenser of truth. A man comes to know the truth by simply listening to and obeying the Church, so if he wishes a deep knowledge of the truth he makes a deep study of all the Church Councils down the ages. Another form of this mistake is found in those who imagine that in their spiritual experience they find truth, whether it be in the form of visions, dreams, or gifts of the Spirit. It is in their experience that they feel they have found the truth and they use it to judge both the Church and the Bible.

The third mistake is to imagine that some of the truth is in the Bible, some in the Church and some in Christian experience, so that total truth is found by adding them together. For example, Roman Catholic teaching before Vatican II implied that the whole truth is found by adding the Bible's teaching to church tradition. And a certain type of Protestant pietism finds truth by adding the Bible to Christian experience. This would be like taking the lenses out of the telescope, examining them and then adding up the findings. To do this would not bring any knowledge of the star. The lenses must be in such a position that the light can shine through them all. The reality is beyond them.

The Holy Spirit brings faith and trust in Christ to birth when we read the Scriptures aware of the fellowship of the Church and with a desire to make what we read real in our own experience.

The interpretation of Scripture

We do not then interpret Scripture by Scripture (which leads to fundamentalism), nor do we interpret Scripture by church tradition (traditionalism), nor do we interpret Scripture by our own personal experience (pietism). We INTERPRET Scripture by the truth to which it leads us. (This is not to say that we should not compare Scripture with Scripture. One part may indeed shed a great deal of light on another. Also, church tradition and our own Christian experience can help us understand parts of the Scripture – but these are not the basic principles of interpretation.)

Of course, even though a man may claim to follow one of these three wrong approaches, this does not mean that the light of Christ cannot reach him. What he thinks he does and what he actually does are not necessarily the same. A man may claim vehemently that he is interpreting Scripture by Scripture, but his life and faith show that really he is interpreting the Scriptures through the One who is the truth.

The correct approach, happily, draws the sting out of the arguments that continue over the exact nature of the inspiration of the Bible. It allows us, like Calvin, to insist that Scripture must be read 'as if God had written it up in the sky', and yet (again like Calvin) to be unperturbed if some of the historical details do not seem to fit together. Because the words of the Bible are not identified with the truth, it is quite in order to examine the text as a historical document; yet because it is uniquely inspired by God for a unique purpose, 'biblical criticism' should never be divorced from the Church and Christian experience. This means, among other things, that biblical scholars should be practising Christians as well as people of sound learning.

The Bible is a wonderful union of the Word of God and the word of man. That is to say, it is the Word of God audible to us because it is written in human language by fallen human beings.

This union of the Divine and human is most fully seen in Christ. In the one person of Jesus God has united himself to our fallen human nature and in it lived a life of perfect obedience without sin. Some theologians have used the analogy of the Person of Christ to try to understand the relationship of the Word of God and the word of man in the Bible.

Knowing God

This relationship of the Divine and human will always be something we cannot fully grasp, but its reality will face us when we read the Bible, allowing it to bring us to faith in Christ.

SUGGESTIONS FOR FURTHER READING

In the Bible Isaiah 42, Psalm 119, John 1

A Book   *The Bible Speaks Again – A Guide from Holland* (SCM)
            How to Read the Bible, by John Goldingay (Oliphants)
            Biblical Inspiration, by Howard Marshall (Hodder & Stoughton)

36

CHAPTER FOUR

The Trinity

God is One – yet in himself a community of love

In the previous chapter we have said that God reveals himself
to man in Christ, his Son, and the bond which unites us on
earth to Christ (now in heaven) is the Holy Spirit. After Jesus
rose from the dead he commanded his disciples to baptize in
the name of the Father, the Son and the Holy Spirit. Does
this mean that there are three Gods? It cannot mean that
because throughout the Bible we have the teaching that God
is One. 'Hear O Israel, the Lord your God is *one* Lord.' This
truth is never compromised in the Bible and therefore we
must hold fast to it. God is One.

Yet when we say that God is One we do not mean he is
lonely. He is not mere monad and never has been. In some
parts of the Bible, God actually speaks of himself in the
plural, and the most common Hebrew word used for 'God' in
the Old Testament is *Elohim*, which is in fact a plural word.
The very personality of God implies that he could not exist
alone. The fact that 'God is love' means that he could never
have been lonely or monad. The eternal love of God is the
love of Father to Son, and the bond of love uniting Father to
Son and Son to Father is the Spirit. In creating man God
created us in families that we might reflect that eternal love in
our own lives. His purpose was also to adopt us into his
family by his Spirit.

In seeking to understand the doctrine of the Trinity,
Christian thinkers have tried to remember that what God has
revealed himself as being towards us (holy love and wholly
love), God is also in himself.

He is Father, not as the projection of earthly fatherhood but as Father of Jesus Christ

GOD IS FATHER. He is Father of our Lord Jesus Christ, and has adopted as his children all who are in union with his only Son.

But how are we to think of his fatherhood? Are we to imagine our experience of earthly fatherhood and then magnify it to infinity in order to understand what we mean by the fatherhood of God? In other words, are we to interpret the fatherhood of God in the light of our experience of fathers here on earth? This cannot be so. One child's father may be a drunkard who treats his family cruelly and unjustly. If we tell that child that God is like a father, then the child will have a completely false idea of what God is like. Even good fathers on earth are not perfect, and so to magnify our knowledge of them to infinity would still give a distorted picture of God.

When the apostle Paul uses the expression 'the Father from whom every family in heaven and earth takes its true name' (Ephesians 3:14) he is implying that it is from the fatherhood of God that we should understand the nature of earthly fatherhood. Through God's self-revelation we come to understand what true fatherhood means, and we should use this as the way to understand the nature of earthly fatherhood.

God is love. Because he is love, God the Father pities his children. His covenant of love is the basis of his unlimited forgiveness, healing mercy, ungrudging generosity, and care for his children. He teaches, corrects, leads and protects his family. Because he is love he is just and righteous in his dealings with those under his care. He exercises his authority for these purposes, and the relationship of his children to him is one of faithful trust, and loving obedience. This relationship is perfectly seen between God the Father and his Son Jesus Christ.

He is Son, revealed in Jesus Christ whose divinity was veiled, but not absent, during his life on earth

GOD IS SON. When we read the gospel stories in openness of heart to receive the Word of God, we are confronted and challenged by the man Jesus and forced on our knees before him. It is God who meets us in Jesus Christ. He is 'before all things' and 'without him was not anything made that was made'. He is the Word of God who 'was with God' and indeed 'is God'. He who has seen him has 'seen the Father'. He and the Father 'are one'.

Such is the teaching of John's gospel. Now this gospel may have been written later than the other three, and some people think it reflects a view of Jesus which is not true to his actual life on earth, but instead is an idea which the Church came to believe about Jesus later on. On the contrary, the other gospels too teach that Jesus is divine as well as human. For example, in Mark's gospel, Jesus openly claims to forgive sins, in the face of his enemies who say that only God can forgive sins. Again, when Peter states 'You are the Christ, the Son of the living God', Jesus accepts the title, and tells the disciples that his Father in heaven has revealed this to Peter. In Matthew 26, when Jesus is accused by the high priests, and asked whether he is Christ the Son of God, he answers, 'So you say' – a phrase which means in effect, 'Yes, although you don't believe me'; and Jesus goes on to quote a saying from the Old Testament which made the Jewish leaders sure he was claiming to be the Messiah, God's chosen one. ('Christ' is the Greek word for the Hebrew 'Messiah'.)

Yet in Matthew, Mark and Luke, Jesus often tries to hide his true identity. Scholars call this the 'Messianic secret'. Why is this? There are two reasons. First, Jesus wished to prevent misunderstanding; there was an underground political movement, called the Zealots, looking for a 'Messiah' to lead them in rebellion against Rome; Jesus was not to be that kind of a leader. The second is a theological reason. Paul in Romans 1:4 teaches that only by the resurrection was the divine nature of Jesus openly declared; similarly, in Acts 13:33, the Old Testament saying 'You are my Son; today I have become your Father' is applied to the resurrection of Jesus. We can illustrate this by saying that in his lifetime Jesus wore his divinity under a veil, in order that we might know he was truly human, flesh and blood like us. Occasionally the veil was lifted, in his transfiguration for example. But when he hung on the cross even his disciples forsook him; who could believe that God the Son could allow himself to be crucified?

And then – he rose again! The veil was finally removed, and today Jesus wears his divinity and his humanity openly and in perfect harmony. John wrote his gospel to lead people to believe that Jesus is divine as well as human, and through believing to share his risen life (John 20:31). So we find in John's gospel accounts of Jesus using the divine name, I AM – the name of God revealed to Moses (written as Yahweh, or Jehovah, or the LORD, in different versions of the Bible), God who was and is and is to come; so Jesus could say to the Jews, 'Before Abraham was, I am'.

He is Spirit, through whom Father and Son come to God's people

GOD IS SPIRIT. In the Old Testament all that is implied in the being of Yahweh is also implied in the one who is called the 'Spirit of Yahweh'. In the New Testament, the Spirit is often associated with the Father and the Son. In Jewish thought, to associate the Spirit in such a way with God is to give the Spirit the same dignity as God. The phrases 'born of the Spirit' and 'born of God' are used interchangeably in the New Testament. In Acts 5 Ananias and Sapphira are condemned for lying to the Holy Spirit, and this according to Peter is the same as lying to God. This also shows that the Holy Spirit is a personal being and not merely an impersonal force. Hence we are warned against 'grieving the Holy Spirit'. Only a personal being can suffer grief. Blasphemy is the sin of giving insult to God either by making oneself equal with him, or taking his name in vain, or giving him any other form of insult. Blasphemy is a sin against God alone. So when Christ warns against the sin of 'blasphemy against the Holy Spirit', he is giving the Spirit of God the honour due to God himself.

When we say that the Holy Spirit is a 'personal being', it sounds as if we are talking about someone with independent personality. This is not so – the Father, the Son and the Spirit are not independent of one another, they are one. This is a mystery which no one can fully put into words. As always, the best place to look for understanding is to Jesus himself, the Word (or 'meaning') of God. Jesus reveals the Father, and Jesus today comes to us with the Father and works among us in the Spirit (John 14).

God is Trinity, in his own being and in his work towards his creation. This is implicit in the Bible

GOD IS TRINITY. So we can see that there is one God only, yet not only the Father, but also the Son and the Holy Spirit are called God. Tri-Theism, the view that there are three Gods, has to be rejected. God is Trinity, said Augustine. It was Augustine of Hippo who gave the doctrine of the Trinity its mature form, especially in the Western Church in the fifth century AD. It will be·helpful here to summarize what he taught.

The word Trinity is not found in the Bible, but the one God who is Trinity, as Augustine says, is found throughout the Bible. Tertullian, one of the early Church leaders, was the first man to use the word. From before Tertullian right up to Augustine men were thinking and writing about the relationship of the Father, the Son and the Holy Spirit. Augustine's formulation has come to be regarded as the standard of orthodoxy in many Christian churches. He accepts that there is one God who is Trinity and that the Father, Son and

41

Holy Spirit are distinct yet are one Divine Being. Nowhere
does he try to prove it. The Bible, he says, proclaims it. We
cannot speak of any one person of the Trinity in isolation.
The three are distinguished in that the Father 'begets' the Son
and the Spirit is 'bestowed'. Augustine wrestled with the
problem of why the Spirit cannot be called 'Son of God' since
he too comes forth from the Father. Augustine's solution is
that the Spirit is not only the Spirit of the Father but also the
Spirit of the Son. He comes forth from the Father *and* the
Son, and is indeed the bond of love between the Father and
the Son. When Jesus prays 'so that the love you have for me
may be in them, and I may be in them', he is referring to the
Holy Spirit.

Unfortunately, the phrase 'and from the Son' (in Latin,
filioque) became a source of conflict between the 'Western'
Church, and the 'Eastern' Church which broke away in the
eleventh century AD. Today most Christians would agree to
say that the Spirit proceeds from the Father *through* the Son.

In the work of God towards his creation they are
distinguished again. For example, the Son becomes incarnate
and not the Father. Augustine does not like the word
'Persons' to describe the Trinity, but he can think of no better
term. In modern English, 'person' can be misleading because
of the Western stress on the 'individual'. God is very much
family! He is not three individuals! (This is why theologians
like Karl Barth have preferred to speak of God existing and
working in three 'ways'.) Human language is inadequate to
describe God who is Trinity, and even though we use many
analogies, these fall far short of the reality. What we see now
is like a dim reflection in a mirror – one day we shall see face
to face.

Some say the doctrine of the Trinity has been invented by
men and is not biblical. Of course, as we said in the first
chapter, truth is not in the Bible as such, but in faith we are
led by the Scriptures to the truth. The Bible does indeed point
us to God who is Trinity however inadequate our human for-
mulations may be.

Even in the story of creation, we see that God creates by his Word and Spirit. God speaks his Word and it is done. His Spirit breathes life into what has been made. In the Old Testament story of redemption, the revelation of redemption is entrusted to the messenger of Yahweh (who is sometimes referred to as the messenger of the covenant). Not in every case does he appear to be a divine Being, but in certain parts of Genesis (16:7, 24:7, 48:16) he not only has a divine name but has divine dignity and power. It may be significant that God appears to Abraham in Genesis 18 in the form of three men; these three men are referred to by the divine name (Yahweh – or the LORD).

The Holy Spirit is given prominence in the Old Testament in connection with revelation and redemption, and is assigned his office in equipping the Messiah for his work (Isaiah 11:2, 42:1, 61:1), and also his people for the response of faith and obedience (Joel 2:28, Isaiah 32:15, Ezekiel 36:26–27).

The New Testament shows us that in Christ's conception and birth he is conceived by the Holy Spirit and therefore called the Son of the Most High. John the Baptist called men to repentance towards God, and to place their faith in the coming Messiah who would baptize with the Holy Spirit. Clearly Father, Son and Holy Spirit are not identical.

In redemption the Father sends the Son to accomplish salvation, and the Father and the Son send the Spirit to apply this salvation to men. From there on believers are baptized in the name (not names) of 'the Father, the Son and the Holy Spirit', whom the Church acknowledges as 'One God for ever and ever'.

It is not necessary to understand the doctrine of the Trinity in order to know God. Far less is it necessary to be able to explain the ins and outs of such a doctrine. However there are two good reasons for studying it. First, we are commanded to love God with all our minds. As our appreciation of the wonderful character of God grows, so will our love, provided that we do not glory in our wisdom, but in understanding and knowing the Lord (Jeremiah 9:24).

Knowing God

Second, Scripture teaches us to be ready with an answer for anyone who asks us to give a reason for the hope we have — a hope not only for ourselves but for the whole universe. Our trust in God the Father for what we do not yet see is based on what he has revealed as God the Son, whose death and resurrection are the great sign of hope at the centre of history. Our union with God the Son is the work of God the Spirit, who awakens faith and brings human life out of chaos into order, and out of bondage into freedom. Our new life in God the Spirit is the gift of the Father through the Son.

SUGGESTIONS FOR FURTHER READING

In the Bible   Isaiah 6, Psalm 23, John 14

A Book   *Mere Christianity*, by C. S. Lewis (part 4) (Fount Paperbacks)
         A Biblical Approach to the Doctrine of the Trinity, by G. A. F. Knight (SJT Papers)

CHAPTER FIVE

The Community of Faith

The Church is a new community, in continuity with the Old Testament people of God

Some of the key verses concerning the Trinity come from Ephesians 3:16–18. Paul asks God from the wealth of his glory to give us inner strength through the Spirit, that Christ 'will make his home in our hearts through faith'. He goes on to ask that we may come to know the love of Christ (which is beyond knowledge), and *together with all God's people* understand its dimensions.

God is not solitary, as in Islamic belief. He is community. Yet the strength of Islamic community life often puts the Church to shame. For Christians are called into COMMUNITY. To be a Christian is to belong to a family, a worldwide family whose history goes back to Abraham, whose head is Jesus Christ.

The knowledge of God is not (or not only) an intellectual understanding. Who knows the mind of the Lord? (Romans 11:34). It is a total relationship. The Hebrew word 'to know' is used of the relationship between a man and woman. The knowledge of God is not the achievement of an individual, it is the gift of God shared among his people, that together we might explore the dimensions of God and give him praise.

Jesus called twelve men to be with him, and to be sent out as heralds of the Kingdom of God. It is sometimes said that Christ never came to found a Church, but to proclaim the Kingdom. That is a misunderstanding. He certainly would have difficulty in recognizing some expressions of the Church down the ages as his own. But that is our fault, not the fault of his teaching. What he did firstly was to call Israel to repent and live as God's people. But Israel rejected his message, and

45

towards the end of his life on earth we find him spending more and more time with the twelve whom he had chosen to be the foundation of a new Israel, so that the Church (in Paul's words) is founded both on the apostles and the prophets of the Old Testament.

Let us pause and look again at the twelve. They formed the first 'school of Christ'. Together they learned to know him as the Messiah, the revealer of God's purpose for his people. Their school was non-competitive, non-academic, because the knowledge of God is for the humble, and not many of the clever and powerful in the world are chosen (1 Corinthians 1:26). But their relationship with God went through a crisis when Jesus died. Could this be God's chosen leader? Then after the resurrection everything began to fit together. And at the Pentecost festival the Holy Spirit was poured out, and the knowledge of God which for the disciples had been external became internal. As those touched by the East African Revival used to say, 'Before, we believed in Jesus because the missionaries told us; now we know'.

Pentecost is sometimes spoken of as the birth of the Church. It would be better to speak of its *new* birthday, for the Church, the people of God, already existed in Israel. Indeed, to begin with the Christians (as they were later called) continued to worship in the Jewish temple as well as sharing fellowship and teaching in their homes. Then came persecution, and in the end the destruction of the temple. But long before that the Church had taken off independently from Israel, surmounting its second great crisis when Gentiles were admitted.

Yet Paul the apostle, Paul the Jew, never ceased to long for the salvation of Israel. Jew and Gentile together are called to honour their Messiah. Christians have persecuted Jews, and even forgotten that Jesus was a Jew. We worship a Jew in heaven! May God grant that as the time of Jesus' return draws nearer, Jew and Gentile may together be ready to greet him.

The Community of Faith

Unity and Church government

The Church is people – but more than a collection of individuals; a community. This means that the UNITY of the Church is not something which depends on the natural qualities and background of its members; rather the unity of the Church comes from its relation to God through Christ in the Spirit. In John 17 we have the prayer of Jesus for his friends. They have eternal life in knowing the Father and the Son. Jesus has shared God's work with them, and he prays that they may be one, as he is one with his Father. Unity is our Lord's desire for the Church.

What kind of unity is this? It is a spiritual unity. But that does not mean it is theoretical, or invisible! On more than one occasion Paul refers to problems between Jews and Gentiles; he insists that we have already been reconciled, racially, in Christ (Ephesians 2:11–18); *therefore* we should be tolerant with one another, seek to preserve the unity the Spirit gives by means of the peace that binds us together. There is (only) one body! (Ephesians 4:2–4).

This is a problem today, especially where churches of different traditions have planted daughter churches in the same town or area. That is not necessarily a disaster – uniformity does not necessarily help the cause of Christ. But what is clearly wrong is that so often these congregations have no real organic relation to one another – they pass as strangers, or with an annual nod. *One* new people (Ephesians 2:15)? Unity is God's gift. We are already one in Christ. But we have to become one in ourselves, we have to express in the real world what we are in Christ.

Part of the reason for the lack of fellowship between churches is the different patterns of GOVERNMENT. There are roughly three models in the New Testament itself:

(a) **The Jerusalem model** This follows the Jewish synagogue pattern, with ruling elders, plus the apostles (who were willing to delegate authority – Acts 6:1–4). Acts 15 describes a church council met to resolve a matter which

47

affected a number of congregations, and shows the organic link between them. Presbyterians are the nearest to this today, with ministers and elders ruling, and the whole congregation meeting for certain limited purposes.

(b) **The Ephesus model** A church founded by Paul, with elders (Acts 20:17), but no 'president' that we know of. In practice in such a congregation a few people tend to emerge as leaders, and one or two may specialize in other functions such as teaching. The local body has to be careful the wrong sort of people don't get to be in charge (Revelation 2:2). The Christian Brethren approximate to this pattern today.

(c) **The Crete model** Titus is in charge of all the congregations of the island. He is to appoint elders (Greek *presbuteroi*) in each town (Titus 1:5) – and two verses on Paul refers to the elder as a bishop! The name bishop (Greek *episkopos*) means an overseer. Perhaps Titus was the first archbishop! The Episcopal churches, such as Roman Catholics or Anglicans, have followed this kind of pattern.

It is not easy for churches of different traditions to unite. Nor is such union an unmixed blessing. Examples of church unions would be the United Church of Zambia and the Churches of North and South India. Union, to be successful, requires that leaders and people are well taught in the Word of God (which calls our traditions into question) and open to the Spirit of God.

New Testament models – body, bride, building

The New Testament has three lovely pictures of the Church:
(a) **The body** Paul devotes a chapter of his first letter to the Corinthians to this theme. By one Spirit we were all (whatever race or background) baptized into one body, which has all kinds of different members, and one head (Jesus Christ). The members have different functions, in worship and in common life, but all belong together and must honour each other.

(b) **The bride** In Ephesians 5, the relation of husband and wife is compared to the relation between Christ and the Church. In Revelation 22:17 the bride of Christ joins with the Spirit in saying to the bridegroom, 'Come'. The Church is called to be pure and holy, that cleansed by her Saviour she might love and honour him.

(c) **The building** A verse (Psalm 118:22) quoted six times in the New Testament refers to Christ as the cornerstone of a building. Peter calls us living stones, and refers to the Church not so much as a finished product but a spiritual temple still being built for service to God. Paul (1 Corinthians 3:9–13) again calls us God's building, this time with Jesus as the foundation. This picture is related to another, that of the Church as a household, or family. It certainly has nothing to do with the appearance of the place where Christians happen to meet for worship!

Note that each of these pictures needs someone to make it complete. The body requires its head. The bride awaits the bridegroom. The building must have its foundation. In every case Christ himself is the centre of God's people; the doctrine of the Church, like every basic doctrine, depends on Jesus Christ as the link between man and God, in the Spirit!

The Church also awaits the end time, when the earth shall be full of the knowledge of the Lord. God's purpose is moving on, and so the Church, like Abraham, continues on the move; we have no permanent home on earth, we look for the city which is to come (Hebrews 13:14). The structures of the Church must be provisional, and if we put down roots of the wrong kind God steps in with kindly judgement, to prod us out of sleep and on to the road again, to be the community of faith.

The purpose of the Church is to be for God, and for the world, until our knowledge is complete

The PURPOSE of the Church is twofold – to be a people for God, and for the world God loves. That is the meaning of holy – to be set apart for God and his service. The Church is a people *for God*, called to worship and adore him, filled with God's Spirit, God the Spirit offering up in us praise to God the Father through God the Son.

Worship is the primary purpose of God's people – to be a living sacrifice. Worship is the offering of our lives to God, and together our praise and thanksgiving, and our common life (Hebrews 13:15–16). Sunday worship must be put in a twofold context, of the worship of our lives here on earth, and the ongoing worship of the community of heaven.

The other great purpose of God's people is to be *for the world*, sent out in mission. 'As the Father sent me, so I send you', said Jesus. Mission is evangelism and service, which belong together. The world has two senses in the Bible. On the one hand, it is the world which God loves, which Christ enters. On the other, it is the world which rejects Christ and opposes the will of God. In the world we have trouble, and so our life is a continual oscillation between engagement and withdrawal for worship and prayer.

The Church often seems weak, and slow to become the people God intends. But God is patient. He bears with us, and encourages us. He has pledged his own Son to make us one day complete, and even now by his Spirit dwells in the Church. To God be the glory in the Church and in Christ Jesus for all time, for ever and ever, even until what we know is complete – as complete as God's knowledge of us.

SUGGESTIONS FOR FURTHER READING

In the Bible   Hosea 14, Psalm 80, Ephesians 2

A Book   *The Household of God*, by Lesslie Newbigin (SCM)
              The Church, by Hans Küng (Burns & Oates)

PART TWO

Man in God's Universe

CHAPTER SIX

Creation and Genesis

The origin of the universe and the limits of natural science

In the past few decades natural science has taken a new interest in the origin of the universe. Although theories change, the prevailing view of astronomers at present is that our universe had a definite beginning in a 'big bang'. If they are right, then the question arises as to what caused the big bang? But this question takes us behind the beginning of nature, and is therefore a 'supernatural' question which natural science cannot investigate.

Even if the universe extended infinitely back in time, or if the big bang was itself the end of an earlier universe which had collapsed upon itself, we still find ourselves asking the same kind of question, why should anything exist at all? (Even if the oscillating model of the universe were correct, there could not have been an infinite series of oscillations – see Steven Weinburg, *The First Three Minutes*.)

Again, when we think of what the elementary building blocks of MATTER are, we are also faced with mystery. We explain the behaviour of a certain substance by the behaviour of the molecules of which it is made up. But how do we explain the behaviour of the molecules? We do so by explaining the behaviour of the atoms of which they are made. But how do we explain the behaviour of atoms? By explaining the behaviour of the protons, neutrons and electrons of which they are made. And so on! But what about the structure of neutrons, protons, electrons, and their interconnecting wave particles? How do we know when we have reached the really elementary structure of nature? If our search for the ultimate atoms of the world never ceases, then we can never give a final answer to the question, 'What is the reason for the scientific laws that govern the universe?' Scientists as such will never be out of work, but will be continually digging ever deeper and deeper. Such a world would be amenable to scientific analysis, but never completely so. There would always be mystery in it, as much as there is today. Again, nature would have forced us to ask questions beyond itself to the Creator himself.

On the other hand, possibly thousands of years in the future, we may discover what we consider to be the final scientific theory of the universe, but that theory would have no explanation whatsoever, and would have to be accepted as the way the world works. Perhaps we would be able to know that at last we had found the original building blocks of matter and energy. But then we would still be faced with mystery because we could not explain how they behave as they do, there being nothing more elementary by which to explain their behaviour. Once again nature would have forced us to ask questions beyond nature.

So whether we are asking the macro question about the origin of the universe, or the micro question about elementary waves and particles, we are forced to recognize that the universe is not in principle self-explanatory.

Genesis and evolution

What about the origin of LIFE and the theory of evolution? Whether we are talking about the evolution of a galaxy, the evolution of the solar system, or the evolution of life on earth, we are saying that out of a relatively chaotic condition order came. For example, the sun poured down its energy upon the earth and through various very complicated chemical processes fuelled by this energy, life began and evolved to the immense complexity and order we see today. But this is in direct contradiction to one of the most fundamental laws of physics, namely the Second Law of Thermodynamics, which says that, in the universe, order will always move towards chaos and not vice versa unless there is some external

54

intelligent interference. Pouring energy into a chaotic system can never produce order, it will always tend to produce more chaos unless the energy and the system are carefully controlled. So if evolution is right, who is the Controller? If evolution is not right, what then?

Christians sometimes talk as if they had to choose between Genesis and evolution. This is not so, for two reasons. First, if the theory of evolution is correct, this simply sheds light on how God created life – it does not tell us whether or not God existed, or why man is here on this planet.

Second, the scientific evidence for the theory of evolution is not conclusive, and comes under fire from scientists of quite different religious views. There is certainly evidence for small changes within a species, but no evidence so far (for example, from the fossil record) for evolutionary change between major species. To introduce another version and call it, for example, 'punctuated equilibrium', simply means that sudden changes took place but we don't know why.

The person who believes in a Creator can be open minded about evolution, but the person who does not want God involved in his origins and his daily life is not free; he is forced to believe in evolution, or interference from outer space, or whatever.

Genesis itself was not written as an ancient (or modern) scientific account of creation. Science by its very methods can only investigate what lies within nature, within the universe. Genesis starts with God, who created space and time which form the boundary of scientific enquiry. The early chapters of Genesis are an inspired piece of theological writing, called 'theology in pictures' by a recent commentator (George Knight). They tell us the answer to the questions that natural science cannot even begin to ask. Science asks 'how?' Theology asks 'why?', 'who by?' and 'for whom?' Theology has been called the queen of sciences, because it is science which has to answer questions from the Bible, not the other way round. Scientists in a nuclear age are more and more aware of this.

The universe was created distinct from God, but dependent on him

CREATION is a word that goes beyond the limits of natural science. Genesis starts, 'In the beginning, God created the universe . . .' (or, 'When God began to create . . .'). The Hebrew word 'create' is used of God alone. Man makes things out of raw materials. God creates freely, without being dependent on anything or anyone. And when he creates, he creates by his Word and Spirit.

All this means that the UNIVERSE, although dependent on God at all times for its life, is not part of God. It has its own order, its own ways. It can be studied; God is not threatened when part of his creation is put under the microscope! The universe, then, is not an emanation from God, nor is God the sum total of all that exists. The universe is distinct from God, having been created by him 'out of nothing'.

It is also dependent upon him as its Creator and Preserver. It is an ordered universe governed by laws of nature. The source of its order and rationality is the Eternal Word of Truth (the Logos of God), through whom the universe was created. Because its order is dependent upon God, its order is not self-explanatory. The universe cannot be fully understood out of itself alone. However, because its order is real order, the universe is open to investigation by man, who can unfold its riches and more and more reveal its hidden structures to the glory of the Creator. This should be the purpose of pure natural science.

When we say that the universe is dependent upon God, we do not mean that God has to keep interfering with it to regulate it. We mean that however far we investigate it, it cannot be reduced to mechanical self-sufficiency. So we reject determinism and fate. In a purely mechanistic universe every event including a human event would have been written in, as it were, from the beginning, and there would be no freedom and therefore no guilt. Reward and punishment would have no meaning.

Creation and Genesis

Insights from modern science

Now let us go on to some points from NATURAL SCIENCE which are at least relevant to what we are saying.

Firstly, modern science does not treat space and time merely as the framework within which natural processes take place. It used to be thought that space and time were absolutes, that objects were merely in space and events merely took place in time and space. However we now know that space and time are not absolutes, but are part of the very subject matter of natural science, and that without objects and events there is no space and no time. Thus we must say that space and time (or more accurately space-time) are (is) part of God's creation. When we say he created everything out of nothing, we mean everything, including space-time itself. (That is why the question 'Who made God?' is silly – it treats God as if he were within space-time and open to investigation by natural science.)

Secondly, quantum mechanics, dealing with the small packets of energy and matter (quanta), have taught us something called the Uncertainty Principle. This in its original form merely told us that our observations of the very small will always interfere with the reality we are trying to examine, so that we can never be certain of what we find. However we now believe that this indeterminism and uncertainty have to do also with objective reality, so that *in principle* we cannot know where an electron (say) is going to be at any moment in time. This seems at least to call in question any idea that all that happens in the universe was written in, as it were, from the beginning. Determinism and fate seem to have lost their hold on the universe.

Man was made in the image of God; the positive Christian view of creation

MAN is part of the total creation and yet also unique. He belongs to nature, and yet he also transcends nature in that

57

God gives him the task of ruling, subduing and caring for nature. Under the authority of God, man has authority over nature. God has breathed into man his eternal Spirit, and in doing so put eternity in him. Man belongs to earth, and yet also to heaven. He is part of creation, and yet he has been made in the image of God the Creator.

What is this 'image of God'? It means, not that man is physically like God, but that he is a moral being, commanded to do as God does. Throughout the Bible, man is exhorted or commanded not just to be perfect, holy or pure, but to be perfect as God is perfect, holy as he is holy, and pure as he is pure. Although man is distinct from his Creator, God does intend him to share his love, his righteousness, his truth, and his mercy. For example, man must love in the same way as his Creator loves; that is, man's love must be self-giving love. This is written throughout the Bible.

Of course we know that man is now sinful. His love, righteousness, truth and mercy have been badly distorted and twisted totally beyond his repair, so that we often see the complete opposites in man, such as hate, deceit and cruelty. Although we can still say we are made in the image of God, it is an image badly spoiled throughout.

Man then was intended to be a wonderful creature indeed, having intimate fellowship with God through his Word and Spirit, reflecting the image of God to the rest of the world, and caring for the world with an authority given by God. Man was the leader of creation, given a scientific nature, able to unfold its riches for the benefit of all creation and the glory of God.

In spite of the evil we now see all around us, the Christian belief stands that all God created was very good. This is in complete contrast to Greek philosophy and Eastern religious beliefs, which teach that the material world is inherently evil or unreal. Paul had to warn Timothy against these views (1 Timothy 4:1–5). God himself affirmed the material world in the incarnation – really entering a real world and becoming real man.

Creation and Genesis

CHAPTER SEVEN

Sin and its Consequences

Sin, Satan and human pride and rebellion against God

Although the Bible gives us such a wonderful picture of man and nature, it speaks in very different terms about things as they are now. We read that the Son of God came into a world of sin and sorrow, and in our humanity died a death for our sins.

The Bible tells us that in our natural condition we are destined to suffer God's anger; that our minds are full of darkness; that we are spiritually dead; that Satan is the prince of this world; and that men are cut off from God by the SIN for which they bear responsibility. The whole world is now in bondage to decay and death.

The full understanding of the sin and fall of man can only come through the Gospel of Jesus Christ in which the anger of God is revealed against all wickedness. The story of Adam and Eve in Genesis is the Bible's account of the origin of man's sin and fall, and the New Testament gives its interpretation of the significance of Adam and his sin.

However, it is clear from Scripture that the origin of evil lies beyond man in the mysterious yet very real and sinister person of the devil or Satan. He is part of the created order, and therefore was originally good. Only hints as to his origin are given. He is only referred to when his person or activity affects man, and is therefore the business of man. Speculation about the details of just who he is and why he turned evil are not for man. The traditional view of him as a fallen angel whose sin was his pride and rebellion may or may not be true. We may have many questions in our mind, but these must remain unanswered for us this side of eternity. We only know what it is our business to know (Deuteronomy 29:29). Satan is the enemy of both God and man.

If the root of Satan's sin was pride and rebellion, so was the root of human sin the same. This is clear from what the Bible tells us about Adam. That ancient serpent who, the book of Revelation tells us, is the devil and Satan, comes to the man and the woman in their paradise, and suggests that they eat of the forbidden tree so that they will be like God. They are already in his image but this does not mean they know as much as God. The forbidden tree is the tree of the knowledge of Good and Evil. Perhaps it is significant that 'knowledge of good and evil' is a Hebrew idiom for 'knowing everything'.

Whatever the correct interpretation of the Garden of Eden story is, it is clear that the root of man's sin is his unbelief, leading to pride and rebellion. He attempted to exalt himself to be as God. This continues to be the root of sin to this day. In the New Testament the sin of Adam is contrasted to the faith and obedience of Christ, who, although being in the form of God, let go of his glory and humbled himself, taking on the form of a human servant, and dying on the cross. The result of his self-emptying was his exaltation. The result of Adam's pride was his fall.

The Fall and its relation to the rest of creation

The FALL of man affected the whole world. If the leader of creation has lost his way, the creation under his authority will suffer too. To add to that, part of God's punishment to man is that the ground is cursed because of him.

At first thought then, we would expect, as we study the past through archaeology, eventually to come to a time when all of nature seems at harmony with itself. And yet we do not find this. All of nature seems to have been 'red in tooth and claw' at all times. What has become of this golden age? There seem to be three possibilities:

(1) First, it is possible that although God created the world good, this did not mean that it was in itself orderly and in

harmony with itself. He created it, giving it to man whose task was to bring it to order and harmony. The task of giving order and harmony to the world was delegated to man and since man fell into sin, the world was never brought into harmony with itself.

(2) Second, it is possible to read Genesis 3 as a parable which describes man as he turns out to be in every age and every situation, and not a story which describes a fall in history. The story itself is obviously symbolic – the question at issue is whether God means us to believe in a historical fall or not. On this view, the 'goodness' of creation reflects God's intention for man, and teaches us to take a positive view of the world. But man rebels against God's plan, and the consequences of his sin are all around us. Genesis 3 of course does not speak about 'sin' – sin is a theological word which sums up the disobedience, the disorder, the disharmony which is later brought into focus by the 'Law'.

(3) The third possibility sounds like science fiction, but is perhaps the most satisfactory. We have already said, on the basis of the doctrine of 'creation out of nothing', that space and time are not eternal absolutes, but part of the created order. We know also from physics that space and time are part of nature, not just the framework in which nature exists. It follows then that since the whole of nature is affected by the Fall, space and time are affected. So the time in which we are living now is fallen time. We cannot escape from the fallen time in which we live, whether in the past, present or future. So however far we go back in time, we are in the very nature of the case still imprisoned in fallen time. If this is right, then it means that the fall of man transcends our space and time, although hinged on to our space-time, being its origin. (Compare the resurrection and new creation – see chapters 9 and 15.)

Man's sin has separated him from God, spoilt his nature and put him and the world under Satan

Man's act of rebellion and pride has had the following three fundamental consequences:

(1) *Man is separated from God* by a barrier of sin and guilt. In Genesis 3 this is pictured as his expulsion from the Garden of Eden. Man, though, knows that he is separated from God, and is not satisfied with his life away from God. Man tries in many ways to reach the now unknown God, and his efforts take many forms, as seen in the variety of religions we have in the world today. Even his religious efforts are tainted with evil, so that what should be good, namely man's religion, is so often spoilt (even what passes as Christianity!) and even in some cases does more harm than good. Man's efforts to reach God are futile. But there is hope because God himself comes and bridges the gulf between himself and man, taking man's guilt upon himself and, in his Son, dying as a sacrifice for our sin.

(2) *Man's nature has been spoilt.* He was created in the image of God, to reflect God's love and holiness, but he has chosen the image of the devil. He is not totally evil – but every aspect of his being is tainted. (That is what is meant by 'total depravity'.) He can still love, but not perfectly. In his spirit (his relation to God) he falls short. In his soul (his self) he is disintegrated. In his body (what he does) he disobeys God. The image of God is still there, but it has been twisted and broken. Man's universally sinful nature is what is meant by 'original sin'. In Christ, the representative man, God has stretched out his hand, touched us in our sin and death, and brought cleansing to our hearts.

(3) *Man and the world have passed into the dominion of the devil.* We do not mean that man is totally demonic, but that he is always under this alien power, even when he is trying to be religious. The power of the devil over man rests in the fact that man has co-operated with him and shares his guilt. Thus the devil can accuse man before God. The word 'devil'

means accuser. Man may ask why God does not cast the devil into the lake of fire now since he has the power to do so. In asking that question man forgets that he shares Satan's guilt, and therefore must share his punishment.

There is a way for man to be set free from Satan's tyranny over us and his oppression of us through our guilt, and that is the mystery hidden from before the beginning of time, but revealed now in Christ who suffered death as a substitute for us, bearing in his own body and soul the full penalty for our sin.

Satan's dominion covers the world. Authority over the world was given to man, but now, in co-operating with Satan, man has betrayed that authority into the hands of the evil one. So Jesus can refer to him as 'the prince of this world', and not contradict him when he says, 'The glory and authority of the kingdoms of the world have been delivered into my hands' (Luke 4:5–6).

However, God, through Christ who was 'slain from before the foundation of the world' for our sin and guilt, has protected and continues to protect the world from the full force of evil. This he will do until the final day of reckoning.

Sin and death

'In the day you eat of it, you will die', says God when warning Adam not to eat of the forbidden fruit. All the three consequences of man's rebellion outlined above must lead to DEATH, death in body and soul. (i) Since God is the source of life, separation from him means death. The spirit of man links him with God through the Holy Spirit, and so separation from God means spiritual death, which leads ultimately to the death of the whole man. (ii) Man's sinful nature leads to greed, fear and war, and so man begins to destroy himself. (iii) Man, being in the hands of his enemy Satan, is threatened with death. The wages of sin is indeed death, as Paul tells us.

Man was made leader of the world and so now, with the

I.C.A.T.–C

fall of man, the world can only continue in chaos. It too falls under the curse that came upon man. It becomes subject to forces that bring pain, suffering and disease. Sickness, death and natural disasters are now built into the very fabric of the world. Apart from the Gospel of Christ our view of man and his world would have to be totally pessimistic.

Yet there is hope for the world in the one who died for man, because out of death he recreated life, rising from the grave. The whole world, as Paul says, is groaning in birth-pangs, waiting for the revealing of the sons of God. The children of God in Christ will be the leaders of the new creation, which is established in the bodily resurrection of Christ from the dead.

SUGGESTIONS FOR FURTHER READING

In the Bible   Genesis 3, Psalm 109, Romans 6

A Book   Calvin's *Institutes* (book 2, chaps. 1–6) (SCM)
               The Parables of Peanuts, by Robert L. Short (Fount
                  Paperbacks)
               The Meaning of the City, by Jacques Ellul (chap. 2)
                  (Eerdmans)

CHAPTER EIGHT

God's Purpose for Man

Our stewardship is spoiled by sin

In Genesis 1, human beings are made in the image of God. What does this mean? It means that they are to be like him in that they rule as God's stewards over nature. Men and women together are to mediate between God and the created order, offering the praise of the creature to God in worship, and continuing to order the world as God wills. We call this responsibility over the world's resources – animal, mineral and vegetable – STEWARDSHIP.

When man falls into sin, his stewardship is spoiled:

(1) Man and woman no longer act in partnership. In Genesis 3, woman leads man into sin, and man blames woman for his failure to take the initiative in refusing to disobey God's Word. In P. T. Forsyth's phrase, there is now 'a sword between the sexes'; man will begin to dominate woman, and the relation between the sexes will involve pain as well as delight (Genesis 3:16).

(2) Work is no longer a delightful task. Man and nature are set in opposition, and throughout the ages he will waste his stewardship, and destroy his environment. The ground will be under a curse (Genesis 3:17); it will be man's enemy, and he in turn will abuse it with pollution and warfare.

The purpose of the Law, and how Jesus fulfilled it

How then is the situation to be controlled before God himself in Jesus Christ comes to put into reverse the process of sin, decay and death (as an early theologian, Athanasius, put it)? How does God want us to live in this sinful world?

Now that is a question about LAW. It is answered clearly in the Old Testament, and quoted by our Lord Jesus: 'Love God . . . and your neighbour as yourself.' In full, we are told to love God with all our heart and soul and mind and strength; that includes using our minds to understand his ways (which is the purpose of this book!). It is put beautifully in Micah 6:8: 'What the Lord requires of you is this: to do what is just, to love kindness, and to walk humbly with your God.'

This verse can be used to illustrate the three purposes Calvin found in the Law: (i) it is a guide for human society, bringing justice; (ii) it shows us how we may live and please God; (iii) it leads us humbly into fellowship with God through Christ – that is, we are unable to keep it and therefore need a Saviour, and the Law itself prescribes sacrifices which point forward to Christ, through whom we are able to walk with God.

Today there are many difficult and challenging ethical questions facing men and women. Concerning abortion, war, racism . . . and some would even claim that by using *man* generically (that is, to refer to human beings of both sexes) the authors of this book are guilty of sexism! In the time of Jesus, religious lawyers made a good living out of moral and legal issues, and Jesus accuses them of dodging the main demands of the Law in favour of legalism. The Church today has the difficult task of guiding members in moral issues, and on occasion taking a public stand on key issues.

What we have to remember, however, is that Jesus did not come to abolish the Law, but to fulfil it. Paul spoke of Christ as the fulfilment of the Law. What does this mean? It means that Jesus did not simply come to give us a great example of love. He himself fulfilled the original purpose of the Law, which was to be a way of life (though by human failure, it never was this.) And so he accuses the Jews, 'You search the Scriptures . . . yet you will not come to me that you may have life' (John 5:39–40). Again he says, 'What God wants you to do is to believe in the one he has sent' (John 6:29).

When we consider man in God's universe, we should focus on Christ. God relates to man through Christ, and man relates to God through Christ. This does not just concern our personal salvation, it concerns the whole of our human life and relationships. Bonhoeffer used to stress that as people we need to relate to one another through Jesus Christ also.

God's purpose in the coming of his Kingdom, to restore man's stewardship and sum up all things in Christ

When Jesus began his preaching, he said, 'Repent, for the Kingdom of heaven is at hand'. God's purpose for man is the coming of the KINGDOM OF GOD, for which Jesus taught his disciples to pray. This kingdom, which Jesus later claims in word and deed as his kingdom also, is in the world but not of the world; it is present, and yet to come. The kingdom is God's rule. How does he rule? Through Jesus Christ (and Part Three of the book will develop this): it is the rule of Father, Son and Holy Spirit. What is important for us to note here is this: a 'greater than Moses' (who gave the Law) is here. In his teaching Jesus claimed a greater authority than Moses. He pointed his hearers right back to the purpose of creation, for example when he spoke about divorce. Jesus came to restore God's original purpose for mankind, and to give that purpose an extra dimension and a new dynamic; man's original task of stewardship (Genesis 1:28) is now bound up with the life of the Son in the Spirit; this will affect the relationship of the sexes (Galatians 3:28), and our relationship to the natural world.

It is often thought that God the Father created and now preserves the world, God the Son redeemed the world, and God the Holy Spirit applies this redemption to man. However, this stark separation of Father, Son and Holy Spirit is a kind of Tri-Theism, and is not found in the Bible.

Paul tells us 'Christ is the first-born Son, superior to all created things. For through him, God created everything in heaven and on earth, the seen and the unseen things . . . God created the whole universe through him and for him. Christ existed before all things and in union with him all things have their proper place . . . Through the Son, God decided to bring all things back to himself. God made peace through his Son's death on the cross and so brought back to himself all things, both on earth and in heaven' (Colossians 1:15–20).

God creates through his Word (John 1:1–3) and his Spirit (Genesis 1:2). Eight times in Genesis 1 we read 'God said . . . and it was so'. This is the Divine Word of John 1:2, who became flesh in the womb of the Virgin Mary, beginning the New Creation. It is the Spirit of God who is actually on earth giving it form and moulding it. He is the breath of God breathing life into his creation, and also breathing new life into those who are dead because of sin, recreating them in God's image. The Spirit is the bond who unites the creation with the Son and through him with the Father.

Creation has a purpose. God not only created through Christ, but *for* Christ. He is the Alpha and the Omega, the beginning and the end. Creation had a beginning and is also moving towards final consummation.

God's covenant of grace, and misunderstandings of this

Christ is therefore the key to God's dealings with the world. And Christ is God's Word of GRACE to man. God's relationship with man was originally intended to be a relationship of grace. That is to say that God gave himself in love and fellowship to man, freely sharing with him his glory, inviting man to respond in faith and obedience. The basis of this relationship is Christ, through whom and for whom all things were created. It is called in Scripture a COVENANT relationship, as God in Christ makes a firm pledge, or covenant, with man.

It might be thought that this doctrine would be accepted by all Christians, but unfortunately there are those who reject it.

In seventeenth-century Scotland, for example, some taught that man's natural relationship to God was only to him as a Judge, and that only a limited number, namely 'the elect', were related to God through Christ. This teaching still has a widespread influence even today.

Basic to this teaching is that originally man's relationship to God was not in a covenant of grace but a covenant of works. Adam could discern the laws of nature, it is said, by the light of reason. God made a covenant of works with him, that if he kept these laws he would earn eternal life. He did not keep the laws, and so failed to gain eternal life. God then chose out of fallen mankind a limited number to whom he would still give eternal life, and this he did through a covenant of grace begun in Abraham and fulfilled in Christ. He sent Christ into the world to die for this limited number only. From this it can be seen that in this scheme Christ's relationship to creation, as expounded in Ephesians and Colossians, has no place.

A truly evangelical theology must insist that there is only one basic covenant between God and man (although it may have many forms), and that is a covenant of grace flowing from the love of God to man in Christ. The Old and New Testaments are two different stages of this one covenant; the New bringing to completion the Old.

The rejection of this truly evangelical doctrine of God and his creation leads to the mistaken idea of limited atonement and also a false pietism which gives no importance to this earth, and finds little meaning in the biblical promise of a new heaven and a new earth in the new creation. Just as the new creation is in Christ, so the first creation was in him too. This is the clear teaching of the Bible, so God's purpose for the whole of mankind through Christ must be the basis of any evangelical compassion and action in the suffering world in which we live.

Living by grace

It is worth while looking at this from another angle, because many Christians are confused about it; they realize they are saved by *grace*, but then think they have to live according to *law*. Yet Christ has set us free from the law (Galatians 5:1)!

In Scripture we see this freedom coming in two stages, and these often correspond to our developing experience. When Jesus comes to Israel, he has first of all to teach them the true purpose of the Law, and its extent. Now the Law of God, given to Israel (and also accepted by most of the world's religions), is 'Love your neighbour as yourself'. Who is my neighbour? Our Lord's parable of the Good Samaritan gives the double answer, my neighbour is both a person in need and someone of another culture and religion. So the command to love has no limits.

Why was it necessary for Jesus to explain this? Because the Jews, like many Christians today, had failed to understand both the context and the purpose of the Law. It was given to a people whom God had rescued from slavery to be a light, a model, a blessing to mankind (Isaiah 49:6, 51:4–5). Israel was to be a holy people, set apart for God's plan of blessing to mankind. The Law, like the Sabbath, was given for man, not the other way round (Mark 2:27).

So we have to learn our responsibility for others, who may not share our culture, our faith, our colour. We have to be 'converted to the world' (not conformed to it!) as well as converted to Christ. But what, second, is the true motive for Christian compassion and service in the world? Is it merely the Law? No, it is the Gospel! God's grace in Christ!

The second stage of freedom comes not from the teaching and example of Christ, but from his death to free us from the Law and his resurrection as the first of a new race. He who wore our human nature in his incarnate life has now redeemed it and offered it, perfect, to his Father and our Father. To be a Christian is to share a new nature with

God's Purpose for Man

Christ. But this new nature does not belong to people of another planet, it is human nature as God means it to be.

SUGGESTIONS FOR FURTHER READING

In the Bible   Deuteronomy 5, Psalm 148, Galatians 3

A Book   *On the Love of God,* by John McIntyre (Collins)
               I Believe in Man, by George Carey (Hodder & Stoughton)
               The Cost of Discipleship, by Dietrich Bonhoeffer (SCM)

73

CHAPTER NINE

The Christian Hope

The Christian hope is cosmic as well as personal, because of Jesus Christ, the new Adam

Christians are often accused of just wanting 'pie in the sky when they die'! Now we do believe in heaven, and in resurrection from the dead; our Lord based his own belief in resurrection on the character of God as the one who said, 'I AM the God of Abraham . . .' (who had already died when that Word came to Moses in Exodus 3:6). Because God has committed himself to his people with an everlasting covenant, death cannot break the bond. We do not base our hope of resurrection on spiritualist 'experiences', or anything like that; but on the Word of God, made clear in the resurrection of Jesus Christ.

However, the Christian hope is more than just a personal hope, it is cosmic. How is this? First, because man is not just an individual, he is a member of the human race. Second, because the future of man is linked to the future of the cosmos. This becomes clear when we study why the Bible calls Jesus THE LAST ADAM.

Modern Western man thinks of man as an individual, doing his own thing. In Africa man finds his identity in relation to others. And rightly so – because the Bible teaches man's solidarity as son of Adam (Acts 17:26), as sinner (Romans 3:23) and as the object of God's love (1 Timothy 2:3–6). Man is not defined by the individual – rather the individual is defined by man.

So in calling Jesus the last Adam, the Bible is saying something about the relevance of Jesus for every man. The Son of God did not just become an individual man, he became man; the word used in John 1:14 means that he shared our human

75

nature *as it is*: not some unfallen human nature, but the humanity we share today.

In Part Three we shall look in different ways at how Jesus has rescued us from sin. Here we look at him as the new Man, and new Adam, who deals with the rebellion and alienation of mankind. Where man in Adam was disobedient, Jesus was obedient. Where man in Adam was proud and self-exalted, the Son of God humbled himself, becoming a servant. He, as it were, put into reverse the course man in Adam was taking. Adam, in a situation of abundant life, brought death into the world. Jesus, in death, gave life back to the world. 'As in Adam all die, so in Christ shall all be made alive.' This is the thought of Paul, especially in Romans 5, Philippians 2 and 1 Corinthians 15.

The eternal Son of God has become our brother man. Because he is Adam, our flesh, he is able to represent us in offering a faithful and obedient life to God. Because he is our flesh, he is able to represent us on the cross and die in our place, bringing cleansing to our human nature which was defiled by our rebellion. And in his human nature, he rose again; the last Adam lives for ever. He has earned the right to eat from the tree of life, and to share its fruit with his brothers.

But as the last Adam, Jesus does more than this! The first Adam was given special responsibility for the creation, symbolized by the Garden of Eden. He had a special relationship with the animal world, symbolized by his naming of the creatures. When Adam and Eve sinned, they were expelled from the garden, and an angel with a flaming sword barred the way back; this symbolized the break between man and nature, which would from then on be man's enemy.

As the second person of the Trinity, the Son of God was involved with the creating of the universe. All things were made through him, and for him (Colossians 1:16). The New Testament identifies Christ with the Word which God spoke in creation (Genesis 1:3); light is created three days before

76

the sun to show that physical light is a sign of everything that belongs to the light – beauty, truth, goodness, all these come not from the sun, nor from human ideas, but from the Light which is still shining in the darkness (John 1:3).

In becoming part of creation as the man Jesus, God in Christ came not only to heal individual men and women, but to heal mankind as a race; and not only to heal mankind, but to heal nature, space and time and everything that belongs to the created universe. That is why the New Testament says that in his resurrection and ascension Christ has risen 'to fill all things', and that he is the Head, not only of the Church but of the human race; and destined to be Head not only of the human race, but of all things (Ephesians 1:10). We do not see man ruling over all these things now, but we do see Jesus . . . (Hebrews 2:8–9).

The new creation is beyond us but we share in it through Christ, by the Spirit

When we look forward to the NEW CREATION through the pages of the New Testament, we see reality, but it is as if through frosted glass or a dim mirror (1 Corinthians 13:12). In a similar way the Old Testament saints looked forward to the first coming of Christ. They saw reality, but could not fit in all the details.

Yet when we look forward to the new creation the things that have been prepared for us will be so beyond our comprehension that in the nature of the case our earthly languages would be unable to cope. We will hear what no earthly ear has heard, and see what no earthly eye has seen, and experience what no earthly mind has imagined. Perhaps the gift of tongues (which will cease then) is a sign of the inadequacy of our earthly languages. The strange yet beautiful imagery of both the Garden of Eden story and the book of Revelation is a similar indication that the space-time of pre-fallen days and the space-time of new creation days are different and more wonderful than our present space-time. Our mathematics can cope with space-time dimensions beyond our experience but our languages and imagination cannot. If we do try to speak of, or imagine, these things, language becomes apocalyptic. We do not understand it, but we do see something as through the frosted glass of vision. So we find similar apocalyptic images in Genesis 2 and 3 and in the book of Revelation.

When all things are made new our present knowledge of God and his creation will pass away because we will have come face to face with reality. That does not mean that our present knowledge is wrong, it is rather that we know only in part. When the perfect comes, the partial will pass away. When we were children, we spoke, thought and reasoned like children, but when we grew up we left behind that way of speaking, thinking and reasoning.

This does not mean that there is no continuity between this world and the first or the next. They hinge into one another. So that even though Adam's first experience of the garden was beyond our history, yet the Fall is part of our history – in one sense the beginning of our history. Also, even though the new creation will be beyond our present space-time, it will touch our present space-time when Christ comes again into our space-time, and 'all eyes see him'.

Even through the frosted glass we do see reality, and there are certain things we can be sure of, such as: the coming of Christ will be sudden and unexpected, there will be a divine judgement, and God's purpose for this era will be complete. For those who know that Christ is their Saviour and friend, the coming of Christ is a promise full of encouragement in a world where God's kingdom seems so much under attack. The Holy Spirit brings us into fellowship with Christ, here and now, so that the believer can say, 'I have been saved'. With Paul he can say, 'If anyone is in Christ, there is a new creation' (2 Corinthians 5:17). The Holy Spirit bears witness with our spirit that we are God's children, and we rejoice in the hope of sharing God's glory. The Spirit which we receive is described by Paul as the down payment made to guarantee a deal.

The Spirit strengthens us to live with faith in this real world. Paul does not say in Romans 8:28 that everything works for the *best* in a perfect world; he says that everything works for *good* with those who love God. There is no *ideal* world except in our imagination – there is a *real* world that God upholds and where nothing can separate us from the love of Christ.

Yet this salvation will be complete only when Christ comes again to renew all things. The book of Revelation includes a vision of a new heaven and a new earth. In Greek, English and most languages, one word 'heaven' is used with two meanings: (a) the sky, stars and all that can be seen from planet earth, and (b) the dwelling place of God and his angels.

But in Hebrew God is never 'in heaven'. He is always 'above the heavens'. So in Genesis 1:1 we properly translate 'the heavens and the earth' by 'the universe' (for which there is no word in Hebrew), since meaning (a) is the only one possible. But in Revelation 21 we need to keep the word 'heaven' in our translation, since meaning (b) is in view, and meaning (a) included figuratively, just as today we use words like 'high', 'up there' of God, not to say that we think he is sitting on a cloud, but that he is beyond our space-time.

Sometimes people criticize the biblical writers for believing in a 'three-storey universe' – God above the sky, man on earth, hell somewhere underground. Actually it would never have occurred to the writers to see this as a problem; they used human language about God very freely (as we have to, of course), but God in his wisdom directed their use by revealing his Word to them; that, for example, is why Genesis 1 uses the same language as the Babylonian creation story, but in a different style, and teaching a very different theology.

Christ will come again finally to reverse the consequences of man's sin

How does the Christian hope of a new creation finally reverse the three consequences of our sin spoken of in chapter 7?

(1) In this world we are reconciled to God by Christ who has overcome our ALIENATION. In the new creation we shall see Christ face to face. The dwelling place of God will be with man (Revelation 21:3). In the new creation heaven and earth will be reunited. Christ himself incarnate is that union of God and man, heaven and earth, in his one person. In the beginning we read of the Lord God walking in the Garden of Eden in the cool of the day. Whatever it means, it means that God's place (heaven) is with man, and man's place (earth) is with God. Only human sin caused the separation. Jesus said the meek would 'inherit the *earth*'. He said of those who are persecuted for righteousness' sake that they would receive the Kingdom of *heaven*. He did not mean that the meek and persecuted would have different destinies! Their destiny is one, namely the new heaven and the new earth.

When Jesus said, 'the kingdom of heaven is in the midst of you' (Luke 17:21), he was anticipating that day. The task of Christ's new people is to be a sign of heaven on earth, pointing forward to the reality of the new creation.

(2) In this world we are made holy for the Master's use, sanctified by the Spirit of Christ who has overcome our DEPRAVITY and the process of DECAY. But we are not yet fully like him: 'When he appears we shall be like him, for we shall see him as he is' (1 John 3:2). At that time our sanctification will be complete. It will affect our whole being, including our bodies. Even in this life 'He who raised Christ from the dead will also give life to your mortal bodies through his Spirit, who lives in you' (Romans 8:11). But the full redemption of our bodies will not take place until the last day, when we will be made like him, the risen and ascended Christ. 'Just as we have borne the likeness of the earthly man, so shall we bear the likeness of the man

80

of heaven' (1 Corinthians 15:49). 'He will transform our lowly bodies so that they will be like his glorious body' (Philippians 3:21).

Two points should be made clear:

(a) We remain real people in heaven – not ghosts. And yet all kinds of changes must take place! The one clue God has given to help us understand this mystery is the risen body of Christ – still human, eating fish, and yet able to pass through doors. Spiritualists ignore the human aspect of future life, and try to experience the life of heaven without the bodily resurrection of Christ, who is the only way. Materialists just ignore heaven altogether. Jesus Christ, true man and God, holds the two together in such a way that our faith can look forward with real hope.

(b) Although in terms of our space-time, those who have already died are still waiting for the return of Christ and the redemption of their bodies, in their death they are released through Jesus Christ from the limitations of this age, and go at once to be with him. So we should not think of our Christian brothers who have died as in a kind of limbo or waiting room; when Paul speaks of those 'who have fallen asleep' (1 Thessalonians 4:13–14), he means that for the Christian death is not a dreadful end, but simply like falling asleep. (The *Good News Bible* translates 'fallen asleep' just as 'died'.) So we rejoice with those who have gone before us to be with Christ in heaven.

(3) In this world we are delivered from the dominion of the devil, sin, and the dread of death, by Christ who has overcome OPPRESSION by evil forces. However, only in the new creation will we be freed from the pressure and presence of Satan, sin and death so that suffering will be no more. Only then will God 'wipe every tear from their eyes. There will be no death or mourning or crying or pain, for the old order of things has passed away' (Revelation 21:4). 'Nothing impure will ever enter it [the Holy City], nor will anyone who does what is shameful or deceitful, but only those whose names are written in the Lamb's book of life' (Revelation 21:27).

I.C.A.T.–D

81

In this life God's people are called to wage war on evil – by seeking to rescue individuals from Satan's power, and to change oppressive social and political structures. Yet we are warned in Scripture not to use the wrong kind of weapons (2 Corinthians 10:3–4). Evangelism should be a loving presentation of the claims of Christ – not a crusade to grab people for our party or point of view. Although political action should indeed be undertaken for the sake of God and man, politics are always ambiguous; if the cause of Christ is identified with one political party or movement (as opposed to the wider cause of justice and peace) this usually rebounds after a while; witness colonialism in Africa or the sad situation in Northern Ireland.

Some kind of exorcism is practised occasionally in most churches. Used with discernment, in the context of medical and pastoral care, it is a witness to the victory of Christ over Satan. The wider warfare against evil in society is waged primarily by prayer and preaching – these are the two great weapons God has given us.

His coming will be sudden, involving judgement. The nation of Israel is a sign of the last days

The new creation is bound up with the COMING OF CHRIST. His first coming was accompanied by great signs of the Kingdom – water into wine, bodies healed, demons cast out, oppressors challenged. At his second coming the new order will be completely established. Jesus will return suddenly and unexpectedly – as clear as lightning, he taught his disciples. Now some teach that these parables (Matthew 24 and 25) are just stories to teach us to keep awake – but no Jew could understand them that way: Messiah *will* come to 'restore the kingdom to Israel' (Acts 1:6) – but not necessarily in the way that we expect. Our task is to be ready, working for the world and its renewal. Neither the Bible nor world history lead us to hope that the Kingdom will come

82

gradually, in a way which can be analysed (Luke 17:20); but we should continue to love our neighbour, to share the Gospel and take an interest in national and world affairs. The promise of Christ's return should make us *more*, not less, interested in the cause of justice and peace. How will our Lord find us when he comes?

Jews and Christians together are waiting for the Messiah; Christians should never despise Jews or treat them as pagans; after all, we worship a Jewish Messiah! Paul makes it clear in Romans 11 that the NATION OF ISRAEL has a special place in the purposes of God in the last days. Even though we do not know the day or the hour when the Son of Man will come again, Jesus told us that we must be on the watch for signs of his coming. One of the most significant signs, we believe, is the nation of Israel. When Jesus said, 'Watch the fig tree', this was an allusion to Israel.

It must surely be significant that after nineteen hundred years the scattered people of Israel actually did return to their own land and regain their ancient city of Jerusalem. It is also significant that Israel is at the centre of conflict in the Middle East. However, this does not mean that we always have to assume that Israel is in the right in any Middle East argument or conflict. This was the mistake that many in ancient Israel made, and it took Jeremiah to recognize the mistake.

The Apostles' Creed says that Jesus will come to judge the living and the dead. God's JUDGEMENT through Christ is another part of the Christian hope. The New Testament makes clear that not all will inherit the kingdom prepared for the righteous from before the foundation of the world. There will be sheep and goats, wheat and weeds, wise maidens and foolish maidens; two grinding at a mill, one taken and the other left; two in a bed, one taken and the other left.

The place of hell in Christian preaching belongs mainly to the warning that those who have already heard of the Gospel of Christ and rejected it, must receive. It must usually, therefore, be a last resort in preaching as something that may make some think again. The power of conversion

83

lies *primarily* in the message of the grace of God.

However, we would be unfaithful to the Bible if we forgot about hell. We should give it just the emphasis it receives in the New Testament, no more and no less. In expository preaching of the Bible, when we come to a reference to hell, we should perhaps merely read what is written and leave it there. No more needs to be said. Whatever hell is, it is the final state of those who have wilfully rejected God's loving plan for them, which he accomplished at infinite cost in the death of his Son for us. What else do we expect him to do for our salvation if we reject the cross?

The whole creation will be renewed, and man will be at peace with God, himself and the universe

The consequence of man's fall was that the whole earth came under the bondage of decay and death. Now that the leader of the earth had fallen, it could only grind on in chaos. So it is not only man who looks forward to his full adoption, but the WHOLE CREATION waits with eager longing for the revealing of the sons of God, when it will be set free from its bondage to decay.

God's purpose for man will be achieved. Christ, our fellow man, is the guarantee of that. Hebrews quotes Psalm 8, which along with Genesis 1 speaks of a glorious purpose for man as priest, prophet and king of creation. But this lies in the future; we do not yet see man as this kind of leader – but we see Jesus, the first of a new creation (Hebrews 2:8–10).

This is one reason why Paul speaks of Jesus as the 'last Adam' (1 Corinthians 15:45). He is the final man, the one who brings to conclusion God's purpose for his creation. In English, the word 'last' means last in time – but both Hebrew and Greek have words with an inner meaning which Christ fulfils. The Psalms refer to truth as the sum/beginning/end/head (*rosh* in Hebrew) of God's Word. Greek has a word *telos* which means end or goal. How appropriate that our Messiah should come into the centre of human history, the one who reveals God as the beginning and the end (Revelation 22:13), the one who is the starter and the finisher of our salvation (Hebrews 12:2).

Under the leadership of man (even a child, as the following passage shows), the whole creation will find harmony with itself and its Creator.

> The wolf shall dwell with the lamb,
> and the leopard shall lie down with the kid,
> and the calf and the lion and the fatling together,
> and a little child shall lead them . . .
> They shall not hurt or destroy in all my holy mountain;
> for the earth shall be full of the knowledge of the LORD
> as the waters cover the sea.   (Isaiah 11:6,9)

This brings us back to the point made in the beginning of the first chapter, that true wisdom consists not only of man's knowledge of God and himself, but also of the whole of nature which God in Christ created and redeemed for our eternal blessing, and his eternal glory.

SUGGESTIONS FOR FURTHER READING

In the Bible   Micah 4, Psalm 118, Romans 8

A Book   *The Apocalypse Today*, by T. F. Torrance (James
              Clarke)
            Theology of Hope, by J. Moltmann (SCM)
            The World to Come and Final Destiny, by J. H.
              Leckie (T. & T. Clark)

PART THREE

Salvation in Christ

CHAPTER TEN

God's Approach

Why Jesus Christ is central

The title claim, *In Christ all things hold together*, is a very big one. Before we start to look at the doctrine of Christ in more detail, here is a way into the whole subject, which illustrates why Christians believe Jesus Christ is unique, and not just one among other religious leaders.

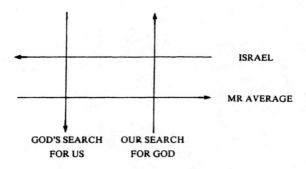

The 'game' of revelation

Without Jesus Christ, the four lines bypass each other. God has indeed shown himself in the history of Israel, but the majority of mankind have no link with that history (and even many Jews today find their history opaque to the reality of God). Again, many people would claim to be searching for God, yet fail to find him (or perhaps find what turns out to be simply their own idea of God).

Various attempts to make sense of life can be illustrated, for example:

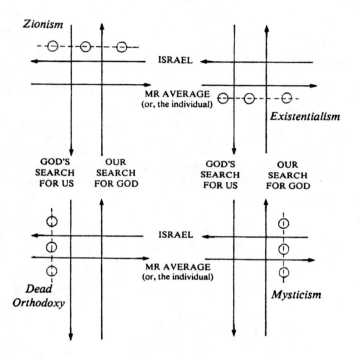

Zionism focuses on the political future of Israel without taking very seriously the rights of non-Jews. *Existentialism* sees life in terms of the individual and his commitment, rather than the destiny of nations. *Mysticism* is preoccupied with our search for God, and *dead orthodoxy* is content to accept a doctrine of revelation without personal commitment. It is possible to plot most philosophies of life on a matrix, using various labels and co-ordinates.

Only Jesus Christ, however, can occupy the centre space with a cross. In him, the history of Jews and non-Jews, Israel and Mr Average, come together, because he is son of Adam

90

as well as son of Abraham (note how the genealogies in Matthew 1 and Luke 3 complement one another).

And in Jesus, God's search for us, and our search for God, are perfectly co-ordinated. So we now redraw the diagram, thus:

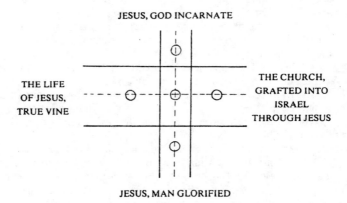

JESUS, GOD INCARNATE

THE LIFE
OF JESUS,
TRUE VINE

THE CHURCH,
GRAFTED INTO
ISRAEL
THROUGH JESUS

JESUS, MAN GLORIFIED

Man's need for salvation requires a sacrificial offering

The need for SALVATION has been described in various ways. There is a gulf between holy Creator and sinful creature. Man is alienated from God. Man is sentenced to decay and death. Man is oppressed by evil. He reaches out for some destiny, some meaning to life, and cannot find it.

Although man without revelation does not know God, and is at odds with himself and with nature, God has still given man light. Calvin described it as light shining through frosted glass, so that man could see by the light, but could not trace the origin of the light. Man is preserved by God, like Cain (Genesis 4:15); evil is limited; and God spares good and bad from final judgement. In his providence (from 'provide') he

91

sends sun and rain upon the just and the unjust (Matthew 5:45). The wheat and the weeds grow together until the final harvest (Matthew 13:30).

Yet God is not indifferent to evil. Because he loves his creation he begins even now to act in judgement against all that spoils it, against injustice and cruelty, against the sin of man which affects both individuals and human society. But as a God of love, he wishes to forgive, and to deal with sin and evil without destroying man. The end of the story of the flood (Genesis 8:20–22) hints at this.

How then is God to work this out? If he merely says, 'Well, it doesn't matter, I'll forgive you', he is not acting as a holy and righteous God, and his forgiveness would in any case find no real point of entry into our lives. Judgement and forgiveness must come together, and they must really touch and enter the life of man.

The place where they are brought together is in SACRI-FICE. 'Without the shedding of blood there is no forgiveness of sin' (Hebrews 9:22). Some people today look on sacrifice as a primitive custom of little importance. On the contrary, sacrifice is of the greatest importance; if it is unfamiliar to modern Western society, there are only two possible reasons:

(1) Evil and its mysterious power is being ignored – often because Satan already has people in his grip, and is perfectly happy if they find him incredible, and choose to believe that 'modern science' has all the answers.

(2) The final sacrifice of Jesus has been accepted by so many people that the original need for it has been forgotten.

One of the ironies of today's world is that some young people in Africa believe that 'Western' science has disproved the reality of evil spirits, while young people in the West, two or three generations away from Christian faith, show an unhealthy interest in black magic and satanism!

Nearly every traditional society is familiar with the idea of sacrifice, usually associated with warding off evil spirits, or of keeping a god well-disposed towards you. But from the time of

Abraham on, we find sacrifice associated with revelation; and under Moses the people of Israel are told to sacrifice in a special way, to the Lord their God at a special place, and not to goat-demons out in the fields like the Canaanites (Leviticus 17:1–7).

However, the sacrifice of an animal has no real power to deal with the sin of man; it merely points forward to another great sacrifice which really does 'take away the sins of the world' (John 1:29). The sacrifice must be at least the sacrifice of a fellow man, because it is man who has sinned. Yet merely to find an innocent man (if one existed) and offer him in our place would be both *unjust* and *insufficient* for the sins of all men. Only one sacrifice can deal with the sin of man, and that is the death of God the Son in our humanity. The wonder of the love of God (Father, Son and Holy Spirit) is that he went to that length to save us, rather than let us take ourselves to eternal destruction. Hebrews chapter 9 explains how the offering of Jesus Christ completes the Old Testament system of sacrifice.

However, if a man rejects, and continues to reject, that self-giving love of God, there is no other sacrifice for sins to save him (Hebrews 10:26). What else does he expect God to do for him? Has not God already done everything? For him eternal condemnation is a reality.

The final offering is Jesus Christ but God's approach to redemption took shape first in Israel

God's approach in redemption took shape in ISRAEL. In Christ, God came to the world, but his drawing near to man in judgement and forgiveness began a long time before the Lord was born into our flesh at Bethlehem. God chose one people out of the world, not because they were any better or more powerful than other peoples, but for his gracious purpose to reveal himself in blessing and salvation to the whole world. His drawing near to them was a very painful

93

process for him and for them. Through reconciling Israel to himself, he would reach all men.

Israel was the chosen people of God, chosen not for its own sake, but for the sake of the whole world. It was not a society formed by human beings, but it was a community called into being by the Word of God. Yet it was also a nation among other nations. It wanted a king. It wanted to worship the gods of the neighbouring peoples and it wanted to trust foreign military alliances. So as God drew near to Israel, Israel began to struggle with itself and with God – the name 'Israel' means 'he who struggles with God' – knowing it was called to be unique and separate, and yet also desiring to be like other nations.

It was this conflict which gave Israel and its God the long ordeal of suffering, alternating between judgement and forgiveness, death and resurrection. Through this suffering God revealed himself and gave himself more and more. As he drew Israel closer to himself through his Word, the remnant of faithful Israel became smaller and smaller. Eventually his Word actually became flesh in Israel, and the mission of Israel was fulfilled in the death and resurrection of this one true Israelite, God's Chosen One, who is the Messiah, Jesus of Nazareth. The fullness of God's self-giving and the fullness of Israel's rebellion are seen in the cross.

There are other titles given to Israel which point forward to Christ. Israel is, for example, God's first-born son, and it was out of Egypt that God called his Son. Another significant name for Israel is 'the servant of the Lord'. Israel was called to be obedient to God. Through the prophets Israel learned that this obedience must touch their real life. It did not just mean ceremonial obedience. From Isaiah 42 to Isaiah 53 we read of the Servant of the Lord who is chosen by God to be a light to all the nations; to open the eyes that are blind; to set free the captives; to bring justice to the earth through the power of the Spirit of God; and eventually to suffer for the sins of all. This suffering is to go as far as death and resurrection. In some passages it is explicitly stated that the servant is

Israel itself, but in other places it appears that the servant is an individual man, especially where it refers to his innocent sufferings and death for the sins of others. Christ himself is the one who gathers up in himself the whole of the mission of Israel. He is the one, as the New Testament tells us, who 'emptied himself and took on the form of a servant' (Philippians 2:7).

Israel presents various models of redemption, fulfilled by Christ

As the Lord drew near to Israel, he brought them REDEMPTION. Redemption ('buying back') in the Old Testament can be seen as a model of the work of Christ to save not only Israel but mankind. T. F. Torrance and others have focused on three Hebrew words:

(1) *Kipper*. This word is used in reference to the system of temple sacrifices God gave the Israelites to atone for their sins, and therefore to show them the way they are again made at one with their God. Literally it means that our sins are 'covered up'. The word is also used for the lid, or cover, of the ark or box which held the stone tablets of the Law. It was the most holy place where God promised to meet his people, overcoming their alienation from him. Corresponding to this is the sacrifice of Christ who covers our sin and is the final meeting place between God and man.

(2) *Ga'al* (or *Goel*). When used as a noun, this word means 'Kinsman-Redeemer', and it is used when God is called 'Redeemer'. When used as a verb it means redeeming by reclaiming what is one's own. It is used for God's redemption of his people out of Egypt and out of exile, but the word emphasizes God's relationship with his people. The Hebrew kinsman had an obligation to buy a relative out of slavery, to avenge the honour of a member of his family who had been killed, and to marry the widow of a deceased relative. God's kinship to Israel is presented as one of his motives for

95

redeeming them. Corresponding to this we can note that in order to redeem men God became kinsman to the human race by taking upon himself our human flesh.

(3) *Padah.* This word means 'to ransom by payment of a price'. It is frequently used in the Old Testament to refer to deliverance from oppressive power, whether it be slavery in Egypt, danger, or death. God delivered his people in the Exodus ('going out'), destroying the power of the oppressor. Corresponding to this is our deliverance by Christ from bondage to sin, guilt, death and Satan.

The way the people of God are to know the will of God is through grace. That is, through the fellowship with God established by his Word and Spirit, men are to know what is required of them. Yet because sin has separated man from God, this intimate fellowship is broken. God in his mercy did not just leave man in total ignorance of what he requires, but gave him the written law. It was added, Paul tells us, because of transgressions. It reflects, as accurately as is possible for a written code, the eternal will of God for man. When fellowship with God is restored in Christ, man is no longer under the written law, but under grace, as was originally intended. The Law is not then discarded, but fulfilled. It can now be said that instead of being written on tablets of stone or paper, it is written on the Christian's heart.

SUGGESTIONS FOR FURTHER READING

In the Bible   Isaiah 53, Psalm 32, Hebrews 9

A Book   Calvin's *Institutes* (book 2, chaps. 9 & 10) (SCM)
Conflict and Agreement in the Church, Vol. 1, by T. F. Torrance (part 2, chap. 5) (Lutterworth)

CHAPTER ELEVEN

Who is Jesus?

The person and the work of Jesus belong together. The Virgin Birth is a sign of God's grace

The *person* of Jesus the Messiah (who is he?) and the *work* of Jesus (what did he do?) belong together. The Son of God became man for us. The Son of God died on the cross. The Son of Man forgave sins. The Son of Man rose from death. To preach the cross, for example, without preaching the one who died there is to empty the cross of its power. Many reject the doctrine that Christ died on the cross as our substitute, because they do not understand that God himself in the person of Christ was reconciling the world to himself. That is to say, it was not just an innocent victim being substituted for us, but God himself taking our place and taking the judgement due to us.

If there was more preaching of the deity of Christ, there would be less doubting of the VIRGIN BIRTH. When the author of life, the one through whom God created the universe, comes into the world, we should not be surprised that a new creation of life takes place, out of nothing as it were. God lays aside the strength of man (Joseph), and the Holy Spirit overshadows Mary, as a sign that the coming of Christ is the coming of grace; Mary responds humbly, a sign of our response to God's Word, 'I am the Lord's servant, may it be to me as you have said' (Luke 1:38). God takes the initiative in our salvation.

This is a miracle. Jesus is to be called the Son of the Most High God (Luke 1:32). He is Emmanuel, God with us. But he is also to be called Jesus – a human name (a form of Joshua), because he is our brother man. Biologically, the child who was born of Mary was no different from us. He had no supernatural genes. Had a surgeon operated on Jesus he would have used no different procedures.

It is interesting that the Hebrew word in Isaiah 7:14 can be translated either as 'virgin' or as 'young woman', although both the Septuagint and Matthew use the Greek word for 'virgin'. This ambiguity reminds us that many of the prophetic statements in the Bible are not to be read as only having reference to one event in history, but that in the Spirit they point forward to greater realities in Christ. That is why debates as to whether or not the Bible is inerrant are so inappropriate to what the Bible really is.

The New Testament says little about the Virgin Birth. But it has much to say about Jesus being the Messiah, the Son of God, the Lord's anointed and so on. The doctrine that Jesus is Son of God does not depend on the Virgin Birth. But the Virgin Birth is an appropriate sign of who he is.

It is important to think of conception by the Holy Spirit in theological, not biological, terms. Muslims, for example, are rightly offended by the view that God did for Mary what Joseph would have done. The *biological* fact, Christians affirm, is that of an empty womb – there was no male seed. And that is as much as we can say, humanly, just as the disciples who approached the grave could only speak of an empty tomb. The *theological* fact which God's Word reveals, is that God is the Father of our Lord Jesus Christ.

The title 'Son of Man' shows both the humanity and the divine purpose of Jesus

The term that Jesus used most often to speak of himself was SON OF MAN. The title would not be unfamiliar to his hearers, because it is found in the Old Testament. In the Old Testament it can merely mean 'man'. The prophet Ezekiel is addressed by God as 'son of man' more than ninety times. The book of Daniel also uses the phrase, though not referring to Daniel, but to a human heavenly figure whose coming kingdom would be everlasting. Later Judaism taught that man was only temporarily lower than the angels, and that the day would come when God would give back to man (represented by Daniel's Son of Man) the authority he was intended to have. And just before New Testament times, a Jewish writing known as the *Similitudes of Enoch* used the terms 'Son of Man' and 'Messiah' interchangeably, which is significant.

Jesus used the term in three different ways. He used it to refer to himself at the time of speaking, for example, 'The Son of Man has nowhere to lay his head'. He used it to speak of his coming sufferings and death, for example, 'The Son of Man must suffer many things'. Thirdly, he used it to refer to his coming again in power, for example, 'And then they will see the Son of Man coming in clouds with great power and glory'.

In Mark 14 we read, 'for the Son of Man goes as it is written of him'. Jesus' words in this chapter about his death refer to a number of Old Testament pictures of the Messiah, for example the shepherd of Israel and the suffering servant of the Lord in Isaiah 53. Indeed the whole of Jesus' life, teaching, death and resurrection brings together all the diverse Old Testament messianic images and combines them in his person.

Whatever the fullness of the meaning of 'Son of Man' is, it means a human being. Jesus, in using the term of himself, is affirming the reality of his humanity.

Christology and early heresies. Kenosis

Jesus Christ is both Son of God and Son of Man. Now a great deal has been written about the exact nature of the relationship between the deity and humanity of our Lord. The word for this kind of study is CHRISTOLOGY. Like the Trinity, the Incarnation cannot be fully grasped by our human minds.

The reason why we must try to explain things further is this: false teachers start to twist or deny the doctrine, and God's people are then caused to doubt the reality and fullness of salvation. That is why Athanasius, an African church leader of the fourth century, was prepared to go into exile five times rather than accept a false slant on the incarnation. Some of the heresies, with their technical names (often after an individual or group), were

Docetism: Jesus was divine but not really human

Ebionitism: Jesus was human but not really divine

Apollinarianism: Jesus was human in body, but his human soul was replaced by the divine Son or Logos, so that he had no human soul

Adoptionism: Jesus was human at birth but was later adopted by God as his divine Son (according to some, at his baptism)

Two other views were at the margin of orthodoxy:

Monophysitism: Jesus had one nature, a divine nature, not two. (An extreme form of Monophysitism was held by Eutychus who taught that Christ's human nature was swallowed up by the divine)

Nestorianism: Jesus' divine and human natures were separate, there being a 'conjunction' but no real union between them

In fact all the above views were condemned by one or other of the great Ecumenical Councils of the first few centuries after Christ. Orthodox teaching said that Jesus Christ was one person in two natures (*hypostatic union*, from the Greek *hupostasis*, a word which means something like our word

100

'person'). In other words, even though Jesus is both the Son of God and the Son of Man, he is not some kind of hybrid half-god, half-man, but one person, fully God *and* fully man. The Son of God united himself to our full humanity (body, mind and spirit; body and soul; or however you choose to describe man).

Not all Christians accepted the majority view, and to be fair, some of the early Councils were manipulated politically. A few churches, mainly in the Middle East, survive as the descendants of the Monophysites and the Nestorians. We should in any case distinguish between orthodoxy and saving faith. The devil is orthodox (James 2:19)! Many people judged to be heretics by their doctrine have been men of deep faith and lovely character. Yet the Church is right to be concerned about its *teaching* and its teachers (James 3:1).

Arianism: The 'Logos' in Jesus was not eternally divine; although the Logos created time, he had a 'beginning' before that

This is a heresy of a rather different kind, a view which also denies the doctrine of the Trinity. Jesus is regarded as the first-born of all creation, not with reference to his resurrection, or his status, but meaning that he had a beginning; he was (when the chips are down) creature, not creator. On some Arian views, such as the Jehovah's Witnesses' today, he is an intermediate being between God and man; other Arian views are more sophisticated and even held by one or two English theologians. Some Unitarians would hold Arian views.

The language of 'one person in two natures' is sometimes regarded as out-of-date. However, no satisfactory alternative has yet been suggested. A more important criticism is that such a description leaves out the dynamic aspect of Christology – that is, that the incarnation of our Lord is a movement in God's plan of salvation. Christ 'emptied himself' and became a servant; he humbled himself as far as a shameful death by crucifixion, and God then exalted him. The Son of God became poor in his humiliation to our level, that we might become rich with him in his exaltation.

But what does Paul mean when he says that Christ 'emptied himself' (Philippians 2:7)? At the time of the Reformation it was taken to mean that Christ, having become man, then emptied himself to death. This is a possible interpretation, but it is more likely that Paul meant the Son of God poured himself out from heaven into our humanity and then into our death.

Kenosis:	The Son of God laid aside his divine attributes of omnipotence, omniscience and omnipresence and assumed all the limitations of human existence

This is a view that was very popular in the nineteenth century. It avoids the philosophical jargon of the early debates on Christology, and it reflects the teaching of the gospels that Jesus was only in one place on earth at any one time and did not know, for example, the date of his return. It safeguards his humanity. However, there are two problems:
(a) The Kenotic theory says, not that the divine Son of God emptied himself out of heaven to unite himself with our humanity, but that in emptying himself of his divine attributes he changed into man. Thus the Kenotic theologians denied the union of the two natures in personal union. They taught that Christ was not the Son of God *united* to man, but the Son of God *changed into* man.
(b) It says that in his exaltation to the right hand of the Father, the man Christ Jesus changed back to his original form, and thus presumably ceased to be man. This means a denial of the doctrine of the permanence of the incarnation, which says that Christ is not man for a little while only, but for all eternity, being now and for ever in the future 'the Man of heaven' (1 Corinthians 15:48).

102

The Incarnation, time and nature

Just because the INCARNATION is beyond the imagination of man does not mean that it cannot be described at all. A generation which has accepted the curvature of space should not reject the idea that God who is beyond time in eternity has united himself with Man in TIME. Questions might arise in our mind as to the divine consciousness of Jesus while still in his infancy. But as C. S. Lewis says (in *The World's Last Night*), we should not attempt to establish a temporal relation between his timeless life as God, and the days, months, and years of his life as Man. The incarnation, says C. S. Lewis, is not an episode in the life of God: the Lamb is slain – and therefore presumably born, grown to maturity, and risen – from all eternity (Revelation 13:8). The taking up into God's nature of humanity, with all its limitations, is not itself a temporal event, though the humanity which is so taken up was, like our own, a thing living and dying in time.

The disciples asked the question, 'Who is this man?' (Mark 4:41), after Jesus had calmed a storm on Lake Galilee. His power over nature amazed and alarmed them. What light does the incarnation shed on NATURE?

God gave nature its rational structure, so that its behaviour is predictable in general terms (though not in every particular) and open to investigation. The doctrine of God's providence means that the universe is always dependent on him, and yet also that God does not keep interfering in such a way that his 'adjustments' become part of the data and so a 'proof' of his existence. So what about the miracles of Jesus?

The miracles of Jesus show on a small scale (in Palestine) and as it were at a different speed the work of God in creation, preservation and redemption of the whole world. It is God who is turning water into wine whenever a grape vine sucks up the rainwater from the ground producing grapes which ferment into wine. Botanists may understand something of how it works, but they cannot manufacture a seed or plant which will do the same thing! When the Son of God walked through Galilee and Judaea as man this whole work of God was seen on a smaller scale and to a more intense degree.

When Jesus turned water into wine, this was a demonstration of his glory – that is, his divine being, the Creator present within space and time in a unique way. When he multiplied the loaves and fishes, this was a sign of man's true mastery over nature being restored, so that the fruits of nature are shared; and also that he as the bread of life offers for ever what nature can only give for a time, being subject to decay. When Jesus refused to turn stones into bread, he showed that nature was not, even for God, something to be manipulated for purposes outside God's will; in nature, corn produces more corn – but stones do not produce bread.

And so these miracles remain signs for faith, and not cudgels to compel the atheist to believe. They present Jesus as one with the Creator, the Lord of Creation, the one whose work is not only to redeem man, but the whole universe, from decay and from death.

It is from this angle that alleged miracles today should be judged. Scientists are generally open to the unusual, remission of cancers and so on, because they know that nature is not totally predictable. More important, does the miracle honour Jesus? If so, then his Spirit is continuing his work (John 14:12–14), and we rejoice in a further sign of the coming renewal of creation. We seek discernment, because not all wonders come from God (Matthew 24:24).

SUGGESTIONS FOR FURTHER READING

In the Bible   Daniel 7, Psalm 27, 1 John 4

A Book   *Christology*, by Dietrich Bonhoeffer (Fount Paperbacks)
              Jesus, God and Man, by W. Pannenberg (SCM)
              **Space, Time and Incarnation*, by T. F. Torrance (Oxford)

CHAPTER TWELVE

A Life of Faithful Obedience

The significance of Jesus' baptism

Christ emptied himself, taking the form of a servant, and was obedient. Our Lord's 'obedience' we could say began when he united himself with our flesh. Another great step was his BAPTISM by John the Baptist in the River Jordan. His baptism was a necessary step to 'fulfil all righteousness'. It was a baptism of repentance and confession, for the forgiveness of sins. Although in himself being without sin, he did not need to repent or confess sin, yet in our humanity, as our representative and substitute, he confessed our sins and as such repented on our behalf. Our own repentance and confession is always inadequate, but in union with Christ through the Holy Spirit, our confession and repentance become real and reach the throne of God, and we are adopted as his children. When Christ was baptized the Father bore witness that 'This is my beloved Son'. He is the only eternal Son of God, but through him we are adopted into the family of God so that in the Spirit we hear the voice of God in our hearts: 'This is my beloved Son, today I have become your Father' (Psalm 2:7).

In his baptism Christ received on our behalf the power of the Holy Spirit and was anointed as Messiah. It was in the Spirit that, so Hebrews tells us, he offered himself as a sacrifice for the sins of the world on the cross.

Baptism was not the end of Christ's obedience. It pointed forward to another 'baptism' with which he was to be baptized – the baptism of blood on the cross. It was there that the work of washing away sin would be completed.

The temptations of Jesus (and the Church)

The obedience of our Lord met another dramatic test in his TEMPTATION by the devil in the wilderness. Two of the three temptations begin with the challenge 'If you are the Son of God . . .' In the temptations Satan is trying to divert Jesus from his mission of suffering and death to an inhuman way of demonstrating that he is the Son of God. So at a later time when one of his disciples, Simon Peter, tries to do the same thing (for different motives of course – Peter was ignorant at that time of Jesus' mission), Jesus turns and says to him 'Get behind me Satan'. Peter had reminded Jesus of the temptation Satan himself had put to Jesus.

(a) The temptation to turn stones into bread was a temptation for Jesus to solve the world's problems and demonstrate he was the Son of God by feeding the hungry and becoming a social reformer. His answer that man does not live by bread alone but by the words of God shows that the root problem is spiritual. Jesus did feed the hungry as we know, but it was not his main work. After he fed the five thousand, they wanted to make him king, but he resisted that, knowing that on the cross his Kingdom would be won. The Church too is tempted to see its main work as social reform; it must show concern for society, but this is not its primary task.

(b) The temptation to jump off the pinnacle of the temple and come to no harm was a temptation to demonstrate that he was the Son of God by astounding the world with miracles. Of course Jesus did 'many mighty works' but these were not his main work. When Herod, and at another time the Pharisees, wanted to see a sign from heaven, Jesus gave them none. He told the Pharisees that the only sign would be the sign of his death, burial and resurrection. The Church too may be tempted to blow its own trumpet, and try to show the world what it can do.

(c) The temptation to bow down to Satan and receive the power and authority of the world was the temptation to use worldly power and the methods of man to bring in the

Kingdom. The Church too, by using the power structures of the world, will never bring in the Kingdom. This does not mean that the Church should take no interest in the affairs of state, nor does it mean that Christians should not go into politics. The power of the Church, however, lies elsewhere. It was after Jesus rose from the dead that he was able to say 'All authority in heaven and earth has been given to me', and also to promise, 'You will receive power when the Holy Spirit is come upon you'.

Christ's life and teaching are part of his redemptive work. His was a real human life; he grew in wisdom and learned obedience

The centre of Christ's work for our redemption is his death. But that does not mean that what went before and after is irrelevant. Far from it! His LIFE and teaching have great significance for redemption. Just as in Israel and in the birth of Jesus, the Kingdom of God is drawing near, so too in the ministry of Jesus the Kingdom comes close. We see our Lord's victory over evil powers in his work of driving out devils. We see his compassion and forgiveness to the sinner throughout the Gospel story. His terrible judgement upon the sins of pride and self-righteousness is seen in his confrontation with the religious leaders. We see his victory over decay and death in his healing miracles as well as a foretaste of the New Creation in his mastery over nature. His relationship as Son to his Father is seen particularly in his life of prayer. His relationship both to God and to man shows him as servant of all. His teaching expounds the meaning of the Kingdom, and his whole life gives us a knowledge of God and ourselves. In the Holy Spirit, when we are brought into union with Christ, we begin to share his ministry, and we know what it means to be 'saved by his life'.

Sometimes Christians begin by trying to follow the example of Jesus. This is not wrong, but the Gospel is more than that; it is good news of forgiveness and union with Christ. Our following is not to be a guilty following from afar, but a joyful life of obedience, because he who united himself with our humanity in his incarnate life is now living in us by his Spirit. Paul speaks of working together with Christ, and refers to his ministry in terms which describe the life of Christ on earth (2 Corinthians 6:1–10).

Christ's life was perfect. And yet it was a real human life. He did not start with any built-in advantage over us (Hebrews 2:17–18). Because of his goodness he felt temptation more, not less, keenly! His life is not only the revelation of God to man, it is the revelation of man to man. Here we see human life as God means it to be, man filled with the Spirit. Christ's perfection, his sinlessness, is this: that he offered his whole life as man to God, perfectly obedient to his Father's will. He grew in his knowledge of God, he learned obedience, even as he grew in body (Luke 2:52; Hebrews 5:8).

The obedience of his incarnation; Jesus' active and passive obedience

We can look at the OBEDIENCE of the Son of God in our humanity in three ways:

(1) *The Obedience of the Incarnation*
The Son of God entered our flesh to become our brother man, and cleanse our fallen human nature. The union of the divine and human in Christ brings cleansing to our humanity. Calvin, in his commentary on Matthew 8:3, uses the cleansing of the leper as a dramatic illustration of this, and especially the fact that Jesus stretched out his hand and touched the leper. He says:

> In the Law, the touch of the leper was contagious, but as there is such purity in Christ he absorbs all uncleanness

108

and pollution, he does not contaminate himself by touching the leper, nor does he transgress the Law. For in assuming our flesh, he has granted us more than the touch of his hand, he has brought himself into one and the same body with us, that we should be the flesh of his flesh. He does not only stretch out his arm to us, but he comes down from heaven, even to the very depths; yet catches no stain thereby, but stays whole, clears all our dirt away, and pours upon us his own holiness. Now, while he could heal the leper by his word alone, he adds the contact of his hand to show his feelings of compassion; no wonder, since he willed to put on our flesh in order that he might cleanse us from all our sins. So the stretching out of his hand was a sign and token of his vast grace and goodness.

In uniting himself to our flesh, he comes down from heaven, 'even to the very depths'. He reaches right down to our sin and death. The full meaning of the incarnation includes his death on the cross. It is through that death that our sinful nature is cleansed, and in union with the man Christ Jesus we are made partakers of the divine nature.

(2) *Active Obedience of Christ*
By this we mean that Christ, by a deliberate act of his will, actively set himself to be obedient to his Father in our humanity. He set his face to go to Jerusalem where he knew death awaited him. He said that no one takes his life from him, but he lays it down of his own accord. He has power to lay it down and power to take it again. In speaking of his active obedience we are not only speaking of his death, but his whole life of obedience as the Son to his Father. This active obedience is therefore his own loving self-offering to the Father in our name and on our behalf.

(3) *Passive Obedience of Christ*
By this we mean that Christ submitted himself to the judgement of the Father on our sin when he identified himself with

Salvation in Christ

us. The Lord laid on him the iniquity of us all. He was treated harshly, but endured it humbly; he never said a word. Like a lamb about to be slaughtered, he never said a word. He was arrested and sentenced and led off to die. It was God's will that he should suffer. Our Lord was obedient to death, even the death of the cross.

SUGGESTIONS FOR FURTHER READING

In the Bible   Numbers 14, Psalm 91, Luke 2

A Book   *The Forgotten Father*, by Tom Smail (Hodder & Stoughton)
               The Life and Teaching of Jesus Christ, by J. S. Stewart (St Andrew Press)

CHAPTER THIRTEEN

The Death of Christ

The meaning of atonement

In this chapter we look at the heart of atonement, the death of Christ. ATONEMENT has two meanings which belong together: a wider meaning of at-one-ment, the bringing of God and man together – and a narrower meaning, that of Christ's work – in particular the cross – to deal with sin. These two meanings are closely connected.

The death of Christ on the cross is not a mechanical sacrifice to appease a cruel God. It is a personal sacrifice in which God himself, through his incarnate Son, is intimately involved. It is only because *God* became man that the sacrifice of Christ is a moral act. It is only because God became *man* that it is effective. So the last two chapters are an essential introduction to this brief study of the cross. Who Christ is comes before what Christ does.

Atonement takes place in time but has an eternal meaning

The New Testament describes Christ as the 'Lamb of God slain before the foundation of the world'. That is to say that although the death of Christ took place in our space-time, quite a long time after the foundation of the world, it also has its place in eternity beyond our space-time. Now, that is easy to say, but it does not mean that it is easy for us to get our minds round it. In fact, since we are confined in our daily experience to our space-time, our minds cannot comprehend what is beyond space-time, nor can our language cope with it. However, we know from the Christian revelation that there is a realm beyond our space-time, and we know from modern science and mathematics that our space-time is not so absolute as we once thought.

What we can say is that the death of Christ happened once and once only, and yet it stands in eternity, spanning the whole of space-time. It is not just those who lived after the time of Christ who are saved on the basis of the cross, but it is also the foundation of all men's salvation. So the writer to the Hebrews can tell us that the death of Christ redeems from sin committed in Old Testament times (Hebrews 9:15). In the Old Testament the people of God really see the grace of God, even though their comprehension of its fulfilment is far from clear. However it was clear enough for Jesus to say of Abraham that he 'rejoiced to see my day, he saw it and was glad' (John 8:56).

Atonement in the Old Testament

In the Old Testament, atonement is always obtained through a sacrifice or a paying of a price. But it is God who provides the sacrifice (Leviticus 17:11). The sacrifice is divinely appointed not because there is any value in the animal victim, but because it points forward to the self-sacrifice of God in Christ on the cross. Two aspects of the atoning death of Christ shown in the Old Testament sacrificial system are, first that the animal victim had to be unblemished (Christ was without sin), and second that the animal victim cost something (atonement is not cheap, sin cannot be taken lightly). 'Without the shedding of blood there is no forgiveness of sin' comments the writer to the Hebrews on the Old Testament system.

Israel's most solemn annual day was the Day of Atonement, when the people of Israel were reminded that all their weekly and monthly sacrifices were not enough to atone for sin. Even at the altar of burnt offering the worshipper stood 'afar off', unable to approach the holy presence of God.

Only on the Day of Atonement did the High Priest (and he

alone) enter by the curtain of the temple, the Holy of Holies, which was considered the very dwelling place of God. There he made sacrifice for the whole people of God, including himself. The curtain was the symbol of the separation between God and man. It was this curtain which, by the hand of God, was torn in two when Christ died.

Note that it was life, not death, which was offered to God in sacrifice. This further teaches us how important it is to hold together the life of Christ and the death of Christ in atonement. God accepts the life of Jesus as an offering which he himself has provided; this is hinted at in the dramatic story of Abraham's journey to sacrifice Isaac (Genesis 22:1–14).

A mysterious part of the early Israelite practice on the Day of Atonement was the sending of a live goat into the desert (Leviticus 16:20–22). The sin of Israel was confessed over the head of the goat, thus symbolically laying it on the goat, which was then banished from the presence of God and man; the name of the goat, 'for Azazel', possibly refers to a desert-demon. The early Church saw this as a picture of Christ on the cross alone doing battle with Satan, and going into Sheol, the land of the forgotten dead, to undo the work of death. Without taking this picture too far, we can see it as a symbol of the mystery of evil, and of the terrible loneliness that Christ endured for us in his pure and holy soul.

In all this, we can see the Old Testament pointing forward to Christ who would fulfil in his threefold office as Priest, Prophet and King the three Old Testament aspects of redemption – redemption by sacrifice, redemption by a kinsman, redemption by the mighty hand of God to deliver from evil.

Atonement in the New Testament

All the New Testament writers agree that the atonement comes from the love of God. It is not that the Son is loving and with great difficulty persuades his Father to give atonement; nor is it that the Father alone is loving and sends a reluctant Son to die for man's sin. The atonement comes from the love of *God*, Father, Son and Holy Spirit. 'God was in Christ reconciling the world to himself' (2 Corinthians 5:19; Colossians 1:19–20).

The death of Christ was not an unfortunate accident, but the will of God. 'The Son of Man must suffer many things,' Jesus said. It was 'by the grace of God' that Christ 'tasted death for everyone' (Hebrews 2:9).

The New Testament speaks of the death of Christ in three important ways – not clearly distinguished, but so dependent on one another that it is difficult to make too much of the differences. (This is as it should be: theology which has everything cut and dried in separate neat little packages is hardly true to the Bible.)

(a) *Christ died as a Sacrifice.* Christ came to die for *sins*, opening the way back to God. His blood was 'shed for many for the remission of sins'. His blood was the 'blood of the covenant'. He was the 'Lamb of God who takes away the sin of the world'. It is 'the precious blood of Christ as of a lamb without blemish and without spot' which is this 'blood of the covenant'. All such New Testament language reminds us of the sacrificial rites of the Old Testament, so Paul can tell us that Christ has 'loved us and given himself for us as an offering and sacrifice to God', and that he is 'our passover' who is 'sacrificed' for us.

(b) *Christ died as our Representative.* Christ died as one representing all humanity. He died for *us*. On the cross he is our representative. 'One has died for all; therefore all have died' is the way Paul puts it. Because he is our brother man he was able to represent the whole human race when he died on the cross (as Calvin pointed out from Matthew 20:28). As our representative, he is able to be our 'Advocate with the Father' now in heaven, because he is the 'atoning sacrifice for our sins' (1 John 2:1–2).

(c) *Christ died as our Substitute.* Not only did he die for us, but he died *in our place.* On the cross he was our substitute.

114

This is not a pagan sacrifice – man seeking to propitiate an angry deity. This is God himself in Christ bearing the penalty for human sin. It is the ultimate depth and mystery and horror of the cross. Words cannot do justice to it – God allowed himself to be hurt at the centre of his own Being by the cross. The Son quoted to the Father words from Psalm 22: 'My God, my God, why have you forsaken me?'

The doctrine of the substitutionary atonement means that we deserve to die; but Christ dies in our place so that we may be freed from the hold of death; and we are set free from the accusing power of the devil. Christ is victor. When the New Testament uses the term 'carrying' or 'bearing' our sins, the idea is one of substitution. 'He himself bore our sins in his own body on the tree.' God has 'made him to be sin, who knew no sin, that we might become in him the righteousness of God' (2 Corinthians 5:21). In this way is the prophecy of Isaiah 53 fulfilled. So also did Caiaphas unwittingly say, 'It is better that one man should die for the people than that the whole nation perish' (John 11:50).

The relevance of atonement

Some of this teaching is strange at first to us. Every age and every culture has its deep concerns, and a sensitive evangelist will latch on to these. For example, in Africa there is a vivid sense of encounter with evil forces, not only evil spirits but the forces of change which threaten as well as promise so much – economic and political forces which easily crush the individual and his family. In the West there is a sense of isolation and despair, anger at unemployment, fear of nuclear war, which has replaced the widespread optimism of the beginning of this century. In every continent, materialism and religions of all kinds compete with one another.

To begin with, we grasp the aspect of the cross (and Christianity) which has an obvious meaning for us. But the cross is not just an answer to our problems, it is the revelation of God! Indeed it may appear foolish to us at first (1 Corinthians 1:18–20)! As we think about the cross, so God by it throws light on other areas of our lives and of the life of the world. We then begin to understand the relevance of aspects of the death of Christ which puzzle us at first. Never despise those parts of the Bible or Christian teaching which seem strange at first. Never think that 'modern man' has outgrown the message of the cross.

The cross is held out to us as a great example of suffering for others (1 Peter 2:21). Textbooks refer to the *moral theory* of the atonement, the view that the love of Christ shown on the cross demonstrates how much God loves us and inspires us to love in return. That is true, but does not take us to the heart of the matter. The cross is also a great victory over evil and Satan in particular. One early view was that Christ had paid the price due to Satan to set us free from his power – this is known as the *ransom theory*; it is movingly illustrated in the children's book *The Lion, the Witch and the Wardrobe* by C. S. Lewis – but Scripture does not teach that any ransom was paid to Satan; there was no collusion between Christ and Satan, rather, the cross was even before the resurrection a great victory over the devil. As many have said, Christ reigns from the cross. This could be called the *victor theory*, and teaches us that the victory of the Kingdom of God is secure, the decisive battle is past, and however thick the smoke of battle, we are on the winning side – nothing can separate us from the love of God.

This chapter, however, has focused on the *penal theory* of atonement; although it is sometimes stated in crude and unbiblical terms, it is here that we find the heart of the mystery of atonement, which has always more to say to us than we can put into words.

The Death of Christ

SUGGESTIONS FOR FURTHER READING

In the Bible   Leviticus 15, Psalm 22, 1 Peter 2

A Book   *The Pattern of Atonement*, by H. A. Hodges (SCM)
               God the Holy Father, by P. T. Forsyth (St Andrew
                  Press)

CHAPTER FOURTEEN

Jesus the Messiah

The meaning of 'Messiah'

In the time of John the Baptist, many in Israel were waiting for a special leader whom God would send. Some of those who looked for such a leader, or MESSIAH, withdrew into the desert and lived in communities. The Dead Sea Scrolls have taught us that different groups were expecting different kinds of Messiah; some a great high priest, others a great prophet, and others a great king.

Orthodox Jews today are still waiting for the Messiah. Although for Christians, Jesus of Nazareth is very clearly the Messiah spoken of in the Old Testament, one of the things which Jews and Christians have in common is the hope that Messiah will come fully and finally to establish God's kingdom.

The word 'Christ', which we use of Jesus, means in Greek just what 'Messiah' means in Hebrew – the anointed one. The people of Israel through their Scriptures had been waiting for the Lord's anointed to bring salvation to them. In the Old Testament the king is most often spoken of as 'the Lord's Anointed'. The title is applied to Saul and to David, and even to Cyrus the pagan Persian king, whom God used for his purposes. In Leviticus the term is also used of the high priest, and at least some of the prophets were anointed. In Isaiah 61 the prophet calls himself 'anointed' by the Spirit of God. The full meaning of Messiah, or Christ, can only be understood in terms of our Lord's threefold office of Priest, Prophet and King, as it is referred to in Reformed theology. Jesus was anointed by the Spirit at his baptism, and at the same time declared by his Father to be his Son, which indicates that the Son of God and Messiah are one person.

119

The threefold office of Christ – Priest, Prophet and King

Priests, Prophets and Kings were the three pillars, as it were, that God had given to Israel: (1) to give it a system of sacrifice pointing forward to the one who would give his own life; (2) to keep it in contact with his Word, which one day would be incarnate; and (3) to provide it with rulers who would deliver, govern and care for the nation until the one came whose kingdom would have no end.

Jesus the Messiah, 'the hope of Israel' (as Paul describes him), fulfils in himself the THREEFOLD OFFICE of Priest, Prophet and King. These offices so overlap and depend on one another that we must never think of one in isolation from the other two.

(1) **Christ our PRIEST** This is most fully expounded in the letter to the Hebrews in which Christ is seen as fulfilling the offering of the High Priest on the Day of Atonement. Thus the Old Testament redemption as priestly sacrifice, and the New Testament view of our Lord's death as a *sacrifice* for sin, is most relevant here. When we think of Christ allowing himself to be a 'lamb led to the slaughter' we are thinking of his 'passive' obedience, but also his 'active' obedience because he is the Priest actively offering himself for our sins. He is Priest as well as victim, for the sins of the world (1 John 2:2).

This can be seen to deal with the problem of man's *alienation* from God. Reconciliation with God is not cheap but involves infinitely costly sacrifice which man cannot provide, but God graciously does provide. Judgement and forgiveness, justice and mercy are brought together in the sacrifice of Christ. God cannot merely pass over that which has spoilt and continues to be the enemy of creation, namely human sin. He must, in his justice, judge it. And yet he also wishes to forgive humanity, because this is his nature too. Some speak of God as if he is sometimes loving and sometimes just, but this is wrong. He is always loving and always just. His love and justice to sinful man can only be brought

120

together in sacrifice, and the only sacrifice that is of worth is the sacrifice of Christ, our offering and High Priest. Through him we are brought back into fellowship with God. The curtain of the temple is torn in two from top to bottom. In Christ the separation between God and man is brought to an end. Christ is the *way* back to God from the dark paths of sin.

(2) **Christ our PROPHET** Moses spoke of a prophet like himself whom God would send from among the people (Deuteronomy 18:15). Moses used to speak to God on behalf of the people of Israel, as the representative of sinners. Jesus, sharing our human nature, one of us, is our *representative* before God. Moses asked that he might be rejected if only the people might be saved from the consequences of their depravity (Exodus 32). God did not agree to that request – but he accepted the self-offering of one greater than Moses, to save us from the *depravity* of our human nature. The work of a prophet was to bring the Word of God to the people. The 'text', as it were, for Christ's work as a prophet is John 1:14: 'The Word became flesh and dwelt among us.' This Word is a cleansing Word because it is the Word of God touching our flesh in its sin and death. When Jesus spoke the word of healing to the leper, 'Be clean', at the same time he stretched out his hand and touched him, becoming, as it were, one with him.

The whole of Jesus' teaching ministry is part of his prophetic office, and yet Jesus himself is the Word of God to man, giving us knowledge of God, knowledge of ourselves and knowledge of creation. He is Prophet, and like prophets before him, he died at Jerusalem. In Jesus and his death and resurrection we know God as loving and righteous; we know ourselves as judged and forgiven; and we know nature as waiting for its deliverance from bondage to decay. Jesus, then, is the bearer of truth and also is himself the Truth, which overcomes our depravity.

(3) **Christ our KING** A good king cares for his people, delivering them from their enemies and ruling them in justice and truth. When he began his ministry, Jesus preached that the

Kingdom of God had drawn near. Some recognized his Kingship and called him 'Son of David' or 'King of the Jews'.

His kingly work is seen most in his destruction of the powers of evil that bind man, namely guilt, the power of sin, and the devil himself. Christ brings deliverance to men, setting them free from bondage to evil in all its forms. The casting out of evil spirits is a prelude to the deep battle with evil on the cross. The strong man's house has been plundered by the Stronger Man.

We saw in chapter 8 that one of the consequences of man's rebellion is that Satan gains power over man (and therefore also over the world) through the guilt of man. The fact that man shares the guilt of Satan means that Satan has a tremendous accusing power over man. He is able to accuse us day and night before the throne of God. The word devil, as we said earlier, means 'accuser'. The foundation of his power is man's guilt. The way for Satan's power to be broken is to break the power of guilt. Christ did this by bearing our sins in his own body on the tree, and therefore dying as our *substitute*. Christ's substitutionary death is the foundation of man's deliverance from the *forces that oppress him* – earthly as well as heavenly – and is most relevant to the office of Christ as King. The mighty hand of God is the weakness of the cross. But then 'the weakness of God is stronger than men'. Jesus, speaking of his death, said 'Now is the ruler of this age cast out'.

Summary and table

To sum up then, we say that Jesus – the Last Adam and Messiah – deals with our rebellion in Adam; brings us back into fellowship with God; gives cleansing to our nature; and sets us free from all that binds us. He gives us life in place of death, and this is what we turn to in our next chapter, which deals with the resurrection and ascension of Jesus to the right hand of God, where he is King of kings and Lord of lords as well as our Advocate with the Father and our great High Priest.

Here is a simple summary of the work of Christ:

Office of Christ	Old Testament Redemption	Obedience of Christ	N.T. Aspects of the Death of Christ	Aspects of the Fall of Man Dealt With
PRIEST	System of sacrifices	Passive obedience	Death as a sacrifice	Alienation from God
PROPHET	Redemption by kinsman advocate	Obedience of the incarnation	Death as our representative	Depravity of human nature
KING	Redemption by the mighty hand of God	Active obedience	Death as our substitute	Man oppressed by guilt and power of Satan

SUGGESTIONS FOR FURTHER READING

In the Bible   Jeremiah 30, Psalm 24, Acts 2

A Book   *Jesus the Messiah,* by William Manson (Hodder & Stoughton)
               Calvin's *Institutes* (book 2, chap. 15) (SCM)

CHAPTER FIFTEEN

The Resurrection and Ascension

The resurrection vindicates Christ

The Resurrection is the VINDICATION OF CHRIST. He is shown to be the Son of God. When one looks at the life of Christ in the gospels, and his claims in word and deed, three possibilities are before us – either he is mad, or he is a deceiver, or he is God. It is the same with the claims the early Christians made for him – either they were victims of an illusion, or they were frauds, or they were telling the truth. The resurrection is the point where man has to decide for or against Christ.

Now there are two ways to approach the resurrection. The first is to consider the historical evidence – important, but beyond the scope of this book. Even so, we saw earlier that God never forces himself upon us through nature. The historian may decide that probably the tomb was empty, but may continue to weigh up this or that explanation without ever coming to say as a believer, 'Christ is risen!'

The second way is to consider the meaning of the event, and that is our task. Christ in his death is victorious over sin and all its consequences. It follows then that his death takes the power out of death. Because Christ defeated sin, he also defeated death. His death is the death of death! Death, having lost its power, could not hold him, so he rose from the dead. The resurrection confirms the power of his death to save from sin.

You can think of the resurrection either as Christ passively being raised from the dead by his Father, or as actively rising from the dead in his own power. In both cases the Holy Spirit is the actual power of the resurrection. When we recognize the fundamental Trinitarian unity between Father,

Son and Holy Spirit, we see that there is no real contradiction in these two ways of considering the resurrection. They are nevertheless two different aspects of his rising.

The first corresponds to his passive obedience. After Christ submitted to the judgement of God upon our sin, God raised him from the dead, giving him a name that is above every name. The second corresponds to his active obedience. Having deliberately set himself to do battle with evil on the cross, he conquered sin and the devil and therefore rose from death. 'I have the power to lay my life down and the power to take it up again', he said (John 10:18).

The tomb is empty, because Christ rose in his body

The resurrection is not just a happy theological idea. It means AN EMPTY TOMB! This is basic to the gospel accounts. Perhaps this is too obvious to state, and yet the bodily resurrection of Christ has been denied by many calling themselves theologians. Others, not wanting explicitly to deny the empty tomb, have questioned its importance for belief. In both cases the resurrection is usually interpreted as something that happened to the disciples' understanding of Jesus and themselves, something in the disciples' minds rather than something that happened to Jesus himself. It is argued that the cross had such a profound effect upon them that after the initial shock they began to understand the full meaning for life of Jesus' death. This so transformed their lives that they interpreted it as if Jesus had risen from the dead.

But this view of the resurrection changes theology into psychology because it centres the resurrection not in Christ but in our human experience. When the objective reality of the resurrection is denied, it is then used to symbolize anything one wants it to symbolize, whether it be a sociological, philosophical, or political theory, or anything else.

Another very different view of the resurrection which nevertheless denies the empty tomb, is that Christ rose 'spiritually' but not bodily. Christ really appeared to his disciples, but only in a spiritual form, his body still being in the tomb. In support of this view it is said that Paul did not explicitly mention the empty tomb, and therefore did not believe in the bodily resurrection. However, for Paul there could have been no radical distinction between soul and body. Paul was a Jew! Salvation is for the whole man. Paul uses the phrase 'spiritual body' to refer to the resurrected body of our Lord. But he could not have written 1 Corinthians 15 without believing in a bodily resurrection.

The resurrection event points forward to the new creation

So, what is the nature of THE RESURRECTION EVENT? When we read the resurrection narratives in the gospels we are clearly faced with the same Jesus who died, and yet in another sense he is different. His body still has the nail prints, yet his disciples do not always recognize him. They are not concerned about where he stays. He no longer seems to live and walk with them as he had done before his death. He appears to them and then disappears. Yet he can still eat and he is still 'flesh and bones'. How can we understand what has happened?

The New Testament speaks of the resurrection of Christ as the foundation of our own resurrection, and indeed of the whole New Creation, the final redemption of our bodies, the new heaven and earth, the new Jerusalem, for which we wait in the future. But as Paul tells us, when we look forward to that, we look as it were into a dim mirror (1 Corinthians 13:12). We see reality ahead but it is not a clear image. We cannot give an exact picture of the New Creation. 'It does not yet appear what we shall be,' John says, 'but we know that when he appears we shall be like him, for we shall see him as he is' (1 John 3:2).

127

The resurrection of Christ, which took place nearly two thousand years ago in our fallen world, belongs nevertheless to the realm of the New Creation, and therefore we cannot understand it fully. But when 'our bodies have been made like his glorious body' then we shall see 'face to face' and 'know as we have been known'. The resurrection of Jesus Christ transcends our space-time, but also takes place within our space-time and is part of our history. The new creation is a new order of space and time, rooted in our present order because Jesus rose wearing our humanity. The post-resurrection appearances show how that the new creation belongs both to our time and to eternity. Our human language is only partly able to describe the resurrection, because it points to the redemption of space and time themselves.

'The whole creation has been groaning in birthpangs until now', Paul tells us, and not only the creation, but we ourselves, who have the first fruits of the Spirit, groan inwardly as we wait for adoption as sons, the redemption of our bodies. In that day the creation will receive its new life. The new heaven and earth will be led by the sons of God; this refers back to the first creation, when man was given authority over the whole earth. This kind of language seems unreal until we grasp who it is that has risen. The person and work of Jesus belong together.

The Ascension

The resurrection of Christ is followed by his ASCENSION into heaven. Very often in the New Testament the resurrection and the ascension are spoken of together. God vindicated Christ by raising him from the dead and exalting him to his right hand in heaven. Matthew and the shorter ending of Mark do not mention the ascension. Only Luke/Acts make the ascension a clear and distinct action of God. And yet the letter to the Hebrews hardly mentions the resurrection, but

128

frequently speaks of Christ's exaltation to the right hand of God. Our Lord goes 'beyond the heavens, into heaven itself'.

The resurrection and ascension are both the result of a single action of God in vindicating Christ after his humiliation (Acts 2:32). Some New Testament interpreters have gone so far as to say that Christ was ascended as soon as he rose. By this they mean that he entered the realm of eternity, having moved out of our space and time as soon as God raised him from the dead. According to this interpretation, the resurrection appearances are to be understood as Jesus stepping out of eternity into time on various occasions, to teach the disciples and also to show them that he had risen as he said.

This interpretation, though attractive and not without truth, does not do full justice to the tradition found in Luke/ Acts that the ascension was a definite event that took place forty days after the resurrection.

Probably the best way to understand the relationship between the resurrection and ascension is to recognize that at the moment of resurrection, Jesus was no longer bound by our space-time. However, it was necessary for the disciples to know that Christ would only appear to them bodily for a short time, and that after the forty days his bodily presence would be withdrawn until his second coming; before then his presence with them would be the presence of the Holy Spirit. It is at the ascension, when Christ commands them to wait for the coming of the Holy Spirit, that the disciples know they will not see him again until he returns in power and glory.

Christ's appearances before the ascension, like the whole incarnation, also teach us that no longer can we make a radical distinction between the world of space-time and 'another world'. God in Christ has bound time and eternity together. Heaven and earth are both part of reality which must now be defined by Christ, not the other way round.

Christ continues his ministry as Priest, Prophet and King, and God's Kingdom grows

At the right hand of his Father, Christ continues and completes his work for us as our Priest, Prophet and King.

(1) **Christ is Priest** 'He has passed into the heavens opening a way into the presence of God, having once and for all made an offering for sin.' This is the main theme of the letter to the Hebrews. Christ now leads our worship, offers our prayers, directs us in our work for God in the world. When Paul speaks of helping to complete what remains of Christ's sufferings (Colossians 1:24), he is identifying himself with Christ in his eternal priesthood, by the Spirit, and thus bearing witness to the cross.

(2) **Christ is Prophet** When we think of Christ as exalted Prophet, we are thinking of him not so much as being God's Word to man, but man's word to God. He is our advocate, as John tells us, before the Father. He has taken our humanity into the very presence of God, and represents man in heaven, speaking on our behalf because he is now eternally united to our humanity. 'There is one mediator between God and man, the *man* Christ Jesus.'

(3) **Christ is King** God 'has highly exalted him and given him a name above every name that at the name of Jesus every knee should bow'. All authority in heaven and earth is his and when he comes again he will come as King and Judge. Those who acknowledge his rule have his eternal protection, and they look forward humbly to the day when they will reign with him over the New Creation.

The ascension means that God is still patient with the world, giving us time for God's will to be done on earth, time for his kingdom to grow. God does not want any to perish (2 Peter 3:9). So the time of the ascended Christ is a time for mission and service, a time when Christians share the good news, pray 'Your kingdom come, your will be done on earth as in heaven', ascribing to God all power and glory because

The Resurrection and Ascension

we have seen his glory revealed in the face of Jesus Christ. And Jesus now presents our human face to the Father.

SUGGESTIONS FOR FURTHER READING

In the Bible   Isaiah 55, Psalm 2, Hebrews 1

A Book   *Space, Time and Resurrection*, by T. F. Torrance (Handsel Press)
Theology of the Resurrection, by Walter Künneth (SCM)
The Ascension of Our Lord, by William Milligan (Macmillan)

PART FOUR

The Life of Faith

CHAPTER SIXTEEN

Christ and Commitment

Conversion to Jesus Christ is not one psychological experience, but faith awakened by the Spirit

CONVERSION is a controversial word, often because it is taken out of its Bible context and misused. It is much easier to demand that others be converted than to take time listening to them and getting to know them. It is worth remembering that Jesus used the word to address disciples, let alone unbelievers (Matthew 18:1–5).

The word means to change, to turn around in attitude (and therefore in action too). The disciples were wondering who would be the greatest in the Kingdom of heaven. And Jesus called a child, saying, 'Unless you change and become like children, you will never enter the kingdom of heaven'. He commended the child for simple faith and a humble attitude. Matthew 18:6 refers specifically to the faith of the 'little ones', who do not need to be converted. This teaches us that it is possible to grow up with a simple trust in Jesus and love for a heavenly Father; such folk never need to be 'converted' in the sense of turning from unbelief to faith. However, many are brought up without any real knowledge of Father and Son; others drift away and have to repent (another word which means 'turn') and be converted afresh to Jesus Christ; still others keep their faith but never grow up spiritually so that their attitude to God is unreal, and they likewise have to change. Becoming 'like a little child' is not the same as being childish. The more we grow up spiritually, the more we understand, the more important it is for us to be child-like with God. This is why many people who are important in the Church still need to be converted.

Our experience of conversion differs according to our

make-up and our circumstances. If our faith has unfolded like a flower turning to the sun, then we shall have no dramatic testimony of conversion. If we have been in open rebellion against God, or harboured pride or resentment, then our conversion may be a painful struggle. The important thing is not how or when we were converted, but whether we belong to Christ and know him.

Christian conversion is conversion to Jesus Christ. Conversion to Jesus Christ is not simply a mental assent to certain doctrines, but a turning to him from the heart so that our attitudes and actions change. Faith is this kind of commitment, faith which works (James 2:14–26).

Faith is commitment. Some resist the Spirit because they are unwilling to repent

Why is FAITH so important?
(a) Because it is the working of the Holy Spirit within us uniting us to Christ. The Spirit brings Christ to us as a Word of love and challenge – the Spirit brings us to Christ as a response of love and obedience.
(b) Because, in Calvin's words, 'so long as we are without Christ and separated from him, nothing which he suffered and did for the human race is of the least benefit to us'.

The exalted Christ sends his Spirit into our hearts and the answer of our hearts is faith. We believe him who justifies the ungodly and so are saved. The bond from us on earth to our heavenly Lord is faith, and this faith has come to birth through the Spirit he has given us. In union with Christ through the Holy Spirit and faith, we are able to repent and receive justification, sanctification and deliverance, and hope for eternity. Some have tried to separate these as if repentance and justification happen first to a man, and then later on sanctification and deliverance, and then finally union with Christ. There are many variations of the order and unnecessary disputes about the meaning of each. However, all the blessings of the Gospel are found in union with Christ who is the foundation of our whole Christian experience. It is his one incarnation, death and exaltation which gives us everything. Everything we need is begun in us in this life and will be brought to completion on the day of the Lord Jesus. Paul uses the little phrase 'in Christ' constantly to describe the Christian life. Because repentance is the result of the Spirit of Christ doing his work in us, many resist him and do not come to union with Christ through faith, because they recognize that this involves turning and learning to say 'no' to self; repentance is dying and rising with Christ! This is a change of life many resist. It is clear from the Bible as well as from common experience that many remain 'without Christ and separated from him' and so are not saved. This is so, even though 'the grace of God has appeared for the salvation of all men' (Titus 2:11). It is not God's fault if we do not turn and commit our lives to him in Jesus Christ.

Commitment is to Christ and his Kingdom

God's Word to man is very clear, 'Repent and believe the gospel', although it comes in different ways and in various contexts. Now the Gospel, the good news, is Jesus Christ himself. But the good news that Jesus himself preached is good news of the KINGDOM OF GOD. There are two reasons for this:

(a) Jesus is the Son in the Father's Kingdom, the one whom the Father honours. (We can also speak of him as the King.) He is the centre of the Kingdom. Yet because his life on earth was one of humiliation, his kingly rule is only seen in his resurrection and ascension. So it is after his death that he himself is preached as the Gospel, and the Kingdom of God is Christ's Kingdom.

(b) Jesus' own teaching about the Kingdom shows that if on the one hand the Kingdom should not be proclaimed without the King, so on the other hand the King should not be preached without the Kingdom. It is all too common for men to be asked to trust a vague spiritual Christ who offers vague blessings but demands nothing. To preach Christ truly is to preach also the Kingdom, to show others that commitment to Christ is a real and costly thing.

Does this mean that we preach the Law, and lay heavy burdens on folk? No, because the Kingdom is a kingdom of grace, grace to sinners, but judgement on those who rebel against God. The Law is simple, it can be read and memorized. We can do everything with the Law except fully obey it! But the Kingdom is elusive. It grows in secret (Luke 13:21). It turns human expectations upside down (Luke 13:29–30). To preach the Kingdom does not condemn listeners to a life of weary effort to put the world right; it shows them what their life and the life of the world is really like, so that faith is real and practical, not a Sunday-go-to-meeting faith.

Other religions, and God's work beyond the Church

Jesus said that the Gospel would be preached throughout the world before the end of the age (Matthew 24:14). This Scripture today is being fulfilled. The Church today is growing faster than ever before, mainly outside Europe.

What about those who die before they hear the good news? They have no opportunity on earth of turning to Christ and embracing his salvation. What about the followers of OTHER RELIGIONS? The Christian response to this is two-fold: to leave God to deal with this issue in his own way, and to seek ourselves to obey the call to share Christ with all mankind, starting with our neighbours. But there are some points to be made:

(1) God shows no bias (Acts 10:34). Cornelius is the example of the honest seeker who responds to the light he already has. What matters, perhaps, is not so much how far we have got at the end of our lives, but what direction we are going in.

138

(2) There is no such thing as the totally honest seeker. Nor is there any perfect religion – certainly Christianity as people observe it falls far short of what God requires. It is not enough to be a 'good Muslim', or a 'good Buddhist' – or a 'good Christian'!

(3) Often we think that we have shared the Gospel, but in fact we have failed to communicate Christ himself. One reason for the failure of evangelism in certain parts of Asia is the presentation of Christ as a 'crusade' instead of as a servant.

(4) The Spirit of Christ, and the Kingdom of God, are at work well beyond the limits of the visible Church. Now Paul speaks of 'truly good qualities which only Christ can produce' (Philippians 1:6). If we come across genuine goodness in someone who does not profess faith in Christ, we should rejoice that Christ is at work 'anonymously' as it were. But we should do more than that. 'Whoever does what is true comes to the light, that the light may show that what he did was in obedience to God' (John 3:21). So we should pray expecting that if his goodness is genuine he will indeed come to the light.

Prayer and obedience

The study of theology is in itself a commitment to Jesus Christ, through whom we dare to speak about God. Without prayer and obedience, theology lapses into an academic subject without challenge to faith today. It is a dangerous thing to become a theologian, one who talks about God (James 3:1)!

Good theology is nourished on PRAYER, and prayer in turn is fed by good theology. John McIntyre writes that the total dimension within which we pray is 'the height and depth of the glory of God's love as Father, Son and Spirit, and the width of the whole world and the whole Kingdom of God throughout time and history'.

If prayer is one of the channels which feeds theology,

obedience is another. Western education has suffered through being unduly based on a Greek model of education. In Hebrew tradition, education combined study of the Law with the practice of a trade. So today there is talk of 'doing theology'. This means working at theology as a response to practical human situations, and is often modelled on the teaching methods of Jesus himself. The danger is that, unlike our Lord, we will import our own ideas and end up with a 'Marxist Theology' or a 'Liberal Theology' or a 'Western Theology' instead of Christian Theology.

The other point to note is that theology is not only a second-hand encounter with God, through reflection on situations and on what other people have said. Theology is first and foremost the humble attempt to meet God and love him with all our mind, so that we speak from God as well as about God. The dangers of pride or despair are ever present. Prayer must be part of the commitment of a theologian.

SUGGESTIONS FOR FURTHER READING

In the Bible   2 Samuel 12, Psalm 116, Mark 1

A Book   *Dynamics of Spiritual Life,* by R. Lovelace
              (Paternoster)
              *Apologetics and Evangelism, by J. V. L. Casserley
              (Mowbray)
              Prayer, by H. U. von Balthasar (part 2) (SPCK)

CHAPTER SEVENTEEN

The Meaning of Grace

God gives himself freely to man in Christ, who died for all

The foundation of the relationship between God and his people is grace. That is to say, he gives himself freely in Christ. We never deserve his blessings, but he pours them out upon us as an earthly father loves to give himself for his children (Matthew 7:11). Even when we are talking only of creation this remains true. God created all that there is through Christ and for Christ and it is he, the Eternal Word, who sustains the universe. Adam and Eve were never in a position where they earned God's favour as a man earns wages. The so-called covenant of works never existed. There has always been only an eternal covenant of grace.

Since God's relationship to all that he has created is through Christ, we must also reject the artificial distinction that is made between common grace for all men, and saving grace for the elect. There is one grace of God and that is his self-giving for us in his eternal Son.

A man may love his fellow with a self-giving love. But would he be prepared to give up his life for the sake of his fellow man if necessary? Probably not, although if it was his close friend he might just do so. But this ultimate self-giving is rare. The self-giving of God went much farther even than this, for even in our state of rebellion against him Christ died for us. It was not just for a few that Christ died, but for 'all' (2 Corinthians 5:15), or the 'many' as the Bible often speaks of all men (Romans 6:15).

Christ died for all because it is the will of God that all be saved (1 Timothy 2:4). Does that mean the Holy Spirit of God does at some time work in each human being? Certainly we must believe that when the Word of God is faithfully preached, the Gospel of Jesus Christ expounded, the Holy Spirit does his work in the hearts of those who hear, for 'faith comes by hearing'. The preaching of the Word is the audible proclamation of the Gospel and through it the Spirit of God brings men to Christ. The sacraments too, when faithfully administered, are the visible proclamation of the same Gospel and so the Spirit of God is able to use them too to unite the receivers to Christ, although this is normally when they are accompanied by the Word.

Both universalism and double predestination distort the Gospel. Grace is not a spiritual substance, but Christ himself

There are two big distortions of the doctrine of grace that have plagued the Church. Firstly there are distortions of what is meant by predestination, and secondly there is a distortion of the meaning of grace itself.

(1) **Double Predestination** Where we part company with both the universalist (who believes that all will be saved) and the predestinarian (who believes that God does not will that all be saved, and that Christ died only for a limited number) is that they both believe that the Spirit of God is irresistible. The universalist says that since Christ died for all, all men, like it or not, will be saved. The predestinarian says that since not all are saved, Christ could not have died for all. Both these views are at fault in their doctrine of God. In saying that his will is irresistible they rob him of his living personality, as if he were only an infinite irresistible force. These views confuse his ability to do as he wills with his supposed willingness to force man's hand and heart.

It was the Pharisees and lawyers who 'rejected the purpose of God for themselves' (Luke 7:30), and they have many followers today. 'Many are called but few are chosen' (Matthew 22:14). Resisting the Holy Spirit (Acts 7:51) is indeed possible, so that faith is not born in the heart of those who continue to 'neglect such a great salvation'.

Salvation by grace alone means that God has not merely met us halfway, but that in Christ he has come right to us into the depths of our sin and death. But even more than this, in our humanity Christ has made our human response to the love of God. We cannot even, for example, confess our sins adequately, but Christ has already done that for us in his baptism. God has done everything for us so that it is not now a question of our own will or effort. God sends the Spirit of Jesus into our hearts to make real in our lives what Christ has done, by giving us faith in him.

A group called the Remonstrants (later known as Arminians) in 1603 produced Five Articles in opposition to the 'Calvinists' whose views prevailed in Reformed Theology in Europe. Calvinists believed that some were predestined to eternal life, and some to damnation. Against this, the Remonstrants spoke of the grace of God 'co-operating' with us. But this was to go too far in the other direction, for it implied that salvation is not entirely by grace. If they had been content with another statement of their own, that 'grace is not irresistible; for it is written of many that they resisted the Holy Spirit', they would have done better. God has done all for us in Christ. If we resist him his Spirit will not always immediately leave us alone, for he is very patient. However, his Spirit will not strive with man for ever. If we keep resisting him, what else do we expect him to do for us? Has he not already done *everything* in Christ and his cross? This is salvation by grace alone – it is salvation by Christ alone.

Predestination is a deep mystery. It is clearly taught in the Bible (e.g. Romans 8:29). Because it overlaps eternity we must not think that human logic can sort it out neatly. That, unfortunately, is what happens with the idea of 'double predestination' – not only the predestination of those chosen by God (the 'elect'), but the predestination of others for hell. The only biblical justification for the latter is Paul's words about God's right to give or withhold mercy at his own pleasure (Romans 9:14–23). In fact Paul goes on to say (a) that the

143

stubbornness in some cases is not permanent (11:25), and (b) that the coming of Christ reveals that in actual fact all people are in bondage to sin and all are objects of God's mercy (11:32).

A fundamental mistake of predestinarians (even Calvin in his later life) is that they make the predestinating decrees prior to, and more fundamental than, the Gospel of Christ. They teach that God elected out of humanity a limited number to be saved *and then* decided to send Christ to die for them alone. Whereas in the New Testament we read that God 'chose us *in Christ* before the foundation of the world' (Ephesians 1:4). In fact Christ himself is the one 'chosen before the creation of the world' (1 Peter 1:20). He is 'my Son whom I have chosen' (Luke 9:35). Election must be interpreted out of the Gospel of Christ and not the other way round. He, the 'Chosen One', fulfilled Israel's destiny as God's chosen people who were not chosen for their own benefit but that blessing might come to the whole world.

(2) **Means of Grace** Salvation by grace alone means salvation by Christ alone, for grace is nothing other than the undeserved favour of God towards us in Christ. The real issue at the time of the Reformation in Europe was not so much that the Roman Catholic Church denied that salvation was by grace alone, but that they had a false definition of grace. For them grace was not so much the undeserved personal favour of God to us in Christ, but some kind of 'spiritual substance' that is infused into man by God to make man better than he would otherwise be. This error is also commonly found in Protestantism too. The Roman Catholic view seemed to be that a man was brought back to God only when so much grace had been infused into his soul that he merited the favour of God. God would impart something into man to make him acceptable. This something was grace, and its flow depended upon, but was different from, Christ. However it had to flow through channels controlled by the Church, in its sacramental system which was controlled by the hierarchy. A man then had to be on good terms with the

Church, in order to receive this so-called grace. So really man had to earn his own salvation by obeying church rules and regulations. The Church was also able to exercise a tyranny over man because it was the Church which controlled the flow of grace.

This teaching, that grace was impersonal substance, led to the belief that there were different types of grace, such as 'actual grace', 'prevenient grace', 'sanctifying grace', 'sufficient grace', each having a different purpose. In fact, all the gifts of God – faith, the knowledge of God, love, joy, etc. – are found in the one grace of God which is Christ himself given to us in the Holy Spirit. All the promises of God find their 'Yes' in him, Paul tells us.

A commonly used phrase which *can* imply the same mistake is 'means of grace', which is used to mean Bible reading, prayer, Sunday worship, the sacraments, etc. If the phrase means that these are channels through which a substance called grace flows to us, then it is misleading. If it simply means that these are the instruments that the Holy Spirit uses to unite us to the one Lord Jesus Christ, then it is permissible.

These instruments of the Spirit are found in the context of the Church. But this does not mean that there is a hierarchy of men or rules which controls the work of the Spirit, but that in the fellowship of believers man most readily finds the Holy Spirit at work through Bible reading, the preaching of the Word, Christian fellowship and the sacraments.

Grace and law – a parable

The basis of God's relationship to us is his grace and our faith. He loves us and gives us his undeserved favour, and in response we trust him absolutely, as a little child does his earthly parents. This is also the basis of our Christian obedience and service in the world. Now where does the Law of God fit into this picture?

Let us imagine a good earthly father who loves his children and whose children love and trust him, and therefore do all that he says, knowing that it is for the benefit of them all. He acts with grace towards them so that they have *faith* in him because of his *grace*. (We will imagine for the sake of this story that there is no mother to look after the children, but only the father.) Sadly, one day the father is suddenly called away and the children are left alone. The father realizes that he is going to be away from his children for a long time and he is concerned about the well-being of the family.

So he sends them through the post a great list of instructions about how they must behave, because without his presence and the presence of his word they will surely bring harm upon themselves and upon the family relationship unless they have rules to instruct them. He tells them that they must paste the instructions high on the wall so that the laws will always be before them. The instructions contain a relatively small number of very important rules dealing with the most important aspects of behaviour, and these are written in very large writing. But under them are written hundreds of other instructions to govern the details of their life. He is afraid that during his long absence they may forget him, so some of the rules require of them that they regularly do something together to remind themselves of their relationship with him, and this they must do at set times. However, most of the regulations deal with their behaviour to one another, and how to look after the family property. He realizes that their relationship to one another should simply be governed by love, but he knows that because their knowledge is far from perfect their love needs to be guided by rules.

The children do their best to follow the rules, but as time passes (even a short time is a long time for children) their memory of their father grows dim, so that when they think of him they can only think of the list of written rules and regulations continually hanging over them. The grace of their father is now forgotten (even though it was in his grace that he sent

146

them the rules) and their relationship to him is only of impersonal law rather than the personal grace of his presence. The laws even become a burden to them, hard to bear, because without his presence they are not easy to follow. They are under law, not grace. The situation goes from bad to worse in that even though the children recognize that the rules are good, still the rules seem to have the effect of making them want to rebel against them as they see them day after day hanging over them. It is almost as if the rules that are good are provoking them to break them, and this makes them feel guilty because they believe their father is a good man.

Eventually a happy day comes. Their father returns and they begin to know him again, and the first relationship of grace and faith is restored. The father takes the great list of rules and regulations down from the wall. When they want to know what to do, they only need to ask him, for his word and presence are now with them. They do not immediately, in their new-found freedom from the written rules, start breaking them. On the contrary, they now see the wisdom of them all. They do not need them written any more, because of the gracious presence of their father. The coming again of their father has fulfilled the laws. His word gives them light to live by.

That is our allegory. Like all allegories it does not exactly describe reality, or else it would not be an allegory. The last paragraph describes the complete restoration of fellowship with God, begun now but completed in the new creation, for only when we see him 'face to face' will we not need the written code *at all*, even though the *basis* of the Christian's relationship with God *now* is grace and faith, not law. The written law is still needed now, however, because 'our knowledge is only partial. But when the perfect comes, then what is partial will disappear' (1 Corinthians 13:9–10).

In reality, the departure of our Father was caused by us (Isaiah 59:2), and in fact it was we who hid from him (Genesis 3:8). The original relationship was never law, but always grace and faith, and this is why we must reject the

147

doctrine that originally there was a 'covenant of works' between God and man.

Our transgression first of all was a failure to continue *trusting* his Word (Genesis 3:1–6) which *then* led us to disobey his Word. That is to say, our sin was a failure of faith; a breaking by us of the grace-faith relationship.

Through Moses, God gave us the written law, which Paul tells us was 'added because of transgressions'. That is to say, it was not there in the original relationship of grace and faith.

Just as the children's personal knowledge of their father grows dim, so a man 'under the law' has little or no real knowledge of God. When he thinks of God he only thinks of law. He struggles with the question 'How can I be sure God will accept me?' In fact, like the children, he finds that the laws which he acknowledges to be good, become an intolerable burden to him and even seem to provoke him to sin, causing him to do what he does not want to do. Sin that is already in his heart uses the law to revive itself, so that his sin actually increases because of the commandment, so that it can be said that 'the strength of sin is the law' (1 Corinthians 15:56). This is the situation that Paul describes in Romans 7 and causes him to cry out, 'Wretched man that I am, who will deliver me from this body of death?'

In the allegory, the father merely returns to the children to restore the grace-faith relationship. But in reality the return is hard indeed. The cause of separation is man's sin, and the restoration of fellowship means that God in his Son must bear our sins on the cross. The restoration of the relationship of free grace and faith is at infinite cost.

Worship and mission

Martin Luther had one burning question before his conversion: 'How can I find a gracious God?' So far we have considered grace as God's giving of himself to man in Jesus Christ, but beyond that looked mainly at how grace affects personal salvation. Yet in chapter 8 we saw that grace has a wider context.

The Meaning of Grace

To share in God's grace is to share in the life of the whole Church in heaven and earth, which lives by God's grace. Grace is the life of Jesus Christ, showing God to man, and man to God. Grace is bound up with the WORSHIP which Jesus offers now to God, and so with our worship in Jesus' name. Grace is the movement of the Spirit, uniting us with Father and Son.

In ancient Israel, the people gathered at certain great festivals. These were for worship, teaching and evangelism (the Feast of Tabernacles, in Zechariah 14:16, is for Gentiles as well as Jews). So today worship has a God-ward and a man-ward direction, as the celebration of grace. Worship and evangelism are linked in the person and work of Jesus Christ.

To share in God's grace is also to share in the ongoing work of God in the world. God sent his Son, and the ascended Christ sends the Spirit. God is a sending God, he loves to give to his creation which he upholds. To share in God's grace, is to share in Christian MISSION (John 20:21). We are sent, not as masters, but as servants, that is as ministers, in the name of Christ. Paul said that he had his own ministry 'by the mercy of God' (2 Corinthians 4:1), preaching Jesus as Lord and himself as the servant of Jesus.

The key minister is Jesus Christ himself – as Priest, Prophet and King he leads his people in their corporate ministry. In the next two chapters we will look at the sacraments, which build up God's people not only for their own sakes, but for their service in the world. In the final chapter we will look again at the Church's ministry.

SUGGESTIONS FOR FURTHER READING

In the Bible   Isaiah 52, Psalm 150, Revelation 22

A Book   *Law and Gospel*, by Roland Walls (SLG Press)

The Life of Faith

God, Grace and Gospel, by Karl Barth (SJT paper)
Theology in Reconstruction, by T. F. Torrance (chaps.
 9 & 10) (SCM)

CHAPTER EIGHTEEN

Baptism

The meaning of sacraments

Sacraments are visible presentations of the Gospel of Christ. In them, God uses simple things like bread, water and wine to present Christ. Roman Catholics have a broader view of their meaning than Protestants, and include other ceremonies under the term 'sacrament' beyond the two which our Lord instituted himself, namely Baptism and Communion (or the Lord's Supper).

A century ago, communion was controversial. It was the source of fierce debate between Protestants and Catholics (and within the Anglican Church). This was because many Protestants thought of sacraments merely as visual aids to the Gospel, and not (in Paul's language about the Old Testament sacraments) as a sign *and seal*. On the other hand, Roman Catholics have largely abandoned the mediaeval view of the sacrament as a channel of grace, and returned to a Christ-centred view of Baptism and the Lord's Supper, so that there is now a surprising measure of agreement between Roman Catholics, Anglicans and Reformed churches on this issue.

Today, Baptism is controversial, for two main reasons.

(a) Many 'Pentecostal' Christians, whether they belong to Pentecostal churches, to house churches or to 'mainstream' churches, hold the view that there is an experience later than conversion, called 'Baptism in the Spirit'. This is regarded as necessary for fully effective Christian life and witness.

(b) A number of people who were baptized in water as infants, choose late on in life to be baptized as believers. This makes other people baptized as infants question whether their baptism is true Christian baptism.

How Baptism in water and Baptism with the Spirit are related

It is indeed true that the Bible speaks of BAPTISM IN (OR WITH) THE HOLY SPIRIT, though not very often. In 1 Corinthians 12:13, Paul speaks of all of us having been baptized into the one body by the Spirit. The other references are in the gospels or Acts, looking forward to Pentecost, the great Baptism with the Holy Spirit. It is easy for Christians to disagree and hold views such as:

(1) Baptism with the Spirit happens at the same time as water baptism.
(2) Baptism with the Spirit happens at conversion.
(3) Baptism with the Spirit happens after conversion.

What has happened here is basically that different people have taken their own experience and turned it into a doctrine, picking up one or two texts from the Bible to justify it. Or they have picked up a text and decided what it means themselves, without a balanced knowledge of the Bible. The view taken in this book is that baptism in water and Baptism in the Spirit do belong together theologically, but are not necessarily experienced at the same (human) time. It is common both with adults and children for God to have given his Spirit before the Church gives water. Cornelius is an example of this (Acts 10). There are also examples when the reverse is true (Acts 8).

The effect of sacraments, involving the relationship of earth and heaven, cannot be neatly parcelled up and labelled. The word 'baptism' has two ideas in it; one is immersion, though the Jews used it for pouring and sprinkling as well, the other is initiation, the beginning of something. So 'Baptism in the Spirit' must refer both to the beginning of the Spirit's work, and to its fullness! This is why the confusion arises. Again, we can speak clearly about Christ, who is the Word of order; but the Spirit is free like the wind.

In view of all this, while individuals will no doubt continue to use the phrase to talk about a particular experience they have had, it seems wise for the Church to refrain from using 'Baptism in the Spirit' to describe something that must happen to Christians after conversion, but to use it as Paul does in 1 Corinthians. The alternative 'being filled with the Spirit' is more helpful in many situations.

Jesus said, 'I have a baptism to be baptized with', referring to the Cross where he was dipped into our sin and death. Through the Holy Spirit we are united with him in his death and resurrection. This is the Baptism in the Holy Spirit. Baptism in water is a dramatic picture and the seal of Jesus' baptism for us in blood and the Spirit's baptism of us into Christ. 'There are three witnesses, the Spirit, the water and the blood; and these three agree' (1 John 5:8).

There are many places in the Scriptures where the Holy Spirit is compared with water, so that Jesus, for example, speaking of the Holy Spirit, can say, 'If anyone thirst let him come to me and drink. He who believes in me, as the scripture has said, "Out of his heart shall flow rivers of living water" ' (John 7:37–39). This is but one example of many in both Old and New Testaments. Thus it is very appropriate that baptism should also be by water as a sign (though not a bare sign) of the true Baptism which is by the Holy Spirit. In fact to many people the word 'baptism' means only water baptism. However it is a pity that this is so, for John the Baptist spoke of the water baptism which he was giving as pointing forward to the greater Baptism in the Holy Spirit which Jesus would give. There is one Baptism, but it has two parts: an earthly part (water) and a heavenly part (the Holy Spirit). Water baptism must not be considered only a picture of the real Baptism, because being a sacrament of the Gospel of Christ, the Holy Spirit is able to use it to bring men to Christ. This is true even though it would be very wrong to tie the Spirit's Baptism down to water baptism alone.

Theologically they must not be separated, however, for they are both part of the one Baptism (Ephesians 4:5). Jesus in his incarnation binds earth and heaven together. Thus being 'born again' is being 'born of water and the Spirit'

153

(John 3:3–5). The Pentecostal churches and the Charismatic Movement have built a separation into their doctrines so that they teach that baptism in water is a sign of receiving Christ in the Spirit, but that Baptism in the Holy Spirit is something entirely separate, to be waited for by those who are already true believers. Thus in their preaching it can sometimes appear that there is not one Gospel but two – the first about Christ and the second about the Holy Spirit. Their argument is that the disciples first knew and followed Christ, but later, on the Day of Pentecost, were baptized in the Holy Spirit. The fault in this argument is that it is impossible to compare the experience of the disciples exactly with our experience, since they knew Christ before his death and resurrection, whereas we only know him after his death and resurrection. However, the question of what happened on the Day of Pentecost is a real question. The Holy Spirit was present in creation and continually with the prophets in the Old Testament times as well as with the disciples before Pentecost. What then is special about the Pentecostal outpouring of the Spirit? The Holy Spirit's presence with men has always been based on the self-giving of God in his Word. That is to say, the presence of the Spirit within man comes from the grace of God which, as we have seen, goes back to the beginning of creation. The self-giving love of God for the sin of man reached its wonderful fulfilment in the incarnation and death of Christ, so that the fullness of the blessing of Christ can now be known and experienced by man. It was this fullness of the knowledge and experience of salvation, won for us at Calvary, which was poured out on man for the first time at Pentecost. It is clear from the gospels and Acts that the apostles only really began to understand the full significance of the death and resurrection of Christ after Pentecost.

Baptism speaks of union with Christ, and cleansing from sin. It presents Christ

Water baptism, in its different forms, is indeed a good picture of Baptism in the Spirit. What does it mean?

(a) Baptism by immersion in water, practised by the Baptist churches and spoken of in Romans 6, shows very graphically that our union with Christ in the Spirit is a dying to sin and a rising to the righteousness of Christ. It is a new life in union with Christ who died, was buried and rose for us.

(b) Sprinkling water for baptism, as is practised in most Reformed churches, or pouring (as in Roman churches), speaks of the cleansing given to us in Christ through the Holy Spirit. It presents Christ not only to the one baptized, but also to the congregation. They can see the Gospel! The biblical foundation for this is Ezekiel 36:25–27.

Above all, baptism speaks of grace. We do not baptize ourselves. We have to be baptized by another; even so we have to accept that Christ died for us while we were helpless in sin (Romans 5:8). Even for an adult, baptism is only incidentally a witness to our faith (although it should take place after profession of faith).

The New Testament takes a high view of baptism, but that is because it takes a high view of Christ. There are two Greek words, *baptismos*, used generally to describe ritual washing, and *baptisma*, used only by Christian writers. In 1 Peter 3:20–22, we are told that baptism (*baptisma*) saves us; the writer then explains that it is not outward washing (*baptismos*) which saves, but the promise made to God from a good conscience. That is why when an adult is baptized he promises to trust in Christ and obey him. Yet which of us can perfectly make and keep such a promise? So Peter goes on to say that baptism saves through the resurrection of Jesus Christ; he alone lived with a perfectly clear conscience, and in the resurrection God the Father showed that he accepted the promise his Son had made in his own baptism. So it is not inappropriate that parents should make a promise on behalf

of their infant children; it is Jesus Christ who stands behind all
of us at our baptism, and it is his promise the Father accepts.

Baptism and conversion

Although theologically water baptism and Baptism in the
Holy Spirit belong together, yet a person is not necessarily
seen to be baptized in the Spirit and in water at the same
time, even though, of course, Jesus himself was. As John the
Baptist poured water on Jesus, so his Father poured on him
(representing the whole of humanity) the Holy Spirit.
However, this pattern is not always reproduced. It is God
alone who knows the right time to give people his Spirit, and
this is not necessarily the same time as man gives water. In
the case of Cornelius and his household, the apostles were
only beginning to understand that the Gospel was for
Gentiles as well as Jews, and therefore God was ready to
pour down his Spirit before Peter was ready to pour water. In
Acts 8, it is possible that the evangelism and teaching had not
been of great enough depth, so that even though the
Samaritan converts were baptized in water, the apostles had
to come down from Jerusalem in order to make them ready
for the coming of the Holy Spirit.

Today the same is true. Many are baptized in water, but
testify that at a later (or earlier!) date they found faith in
Christ through the Holy Spirit. This applies even to those
baptized in water as adults. It applies also to little children
baptized but not brought up in faith and knowledge of Christ.
It applies even to children of devout Christian parents,
especially when they do not believe it possible for the Spirit of
Christ to dwell in little children. Such children may be
brought up in a Christian 'atmosphere' and yet not be
brought up in faith. Their parents' prayer for them is not that
the Lord will be with them now in the fullness of his grace,
but only at some future date when they have reached the age
of responsibility. Yet we read in the New Testament that

John the Baptist was filled with the Spirit even from his mother's womb.

Water baptism is appropriate wherever there is an openness of heart to the things of the Spirit of Christ. It is abundantly clear from the New Testament that this applies not only to adults, but to the families of Christian adults. The way for God to work on little ones is through the parents. If the parents are open to the Gospel, then it is appropriate that the children are baptized in water. The water has no power in itself, but is a witness and earthly seal, ordained by God, to what God has already begun to do, and will continue to do, in the lives of the children for whom the parents and the whole local church are praying. Augustine even said, 'We baptize children in order that they may be converted'.

Infant baptism

Why do so many Christian churches baptize infants? Some would object that you must have faith to be baptized, infants do not have faith, and therefore they should not be baptized. Now, even supposing that infants cannot have faith, the New Testament never lays down faith as a prior *condition* of every baptism; it assumes that they are linked, but in practice faith may come before or after baptism. The baptisms recorded in the New Testament are those of first generation Christians; we are not told what happened to their children. So we have to go by the general teaching of Scripture, and the meaning of baptism as a sacrament of the Gospel.

(1) The Church is founded on the apostles *and prophets,* with Christ as the cornerstone (Ephesians 2:20). That suggests, not only that Christ is the focus of *both* Testaments, but that the Old Testament Church operated on the same basis as the New, grace – and therefore we expect Old and New Testament sacraments to operate on the same basis. Circumcision is replaced by baptism, and Passover by the Lord's Supper. Circumcision was given to first generation believers and to

their children (Genesis 17), therefore baptism should be treated in the same way – though extended to women as well as men since in Christ there is no longer male or female. In Colossians 2:11–12 Paul makes this link between circumcision and baptism directly.

(2) The Church is described as the household of faith in the New Testament. The word 'household' had for Jews and Greeks a definite meaning – it included children, slaves, even friends of the family. So when adults are said to be baptized along with their household (Acts 16:15 and 33; 1 Corinthians 1:16), the natural meaning is that infants would be included if there were any.

It is probable that baptismal practice varied in the early Church. Theologically, it is the one baptism of Christ (*baptisma*, Ephesians 4:5) that unites us, not the rite (*baptismos*) itself. And yet, just as Jews could not be circumcised a second time, so there is no hint that Christians might be baptized twice. If the meaning of baptism is that Christ died to wash away our sin before we were even born, we can rejoice in our baptism, whether it took place in infant or adult life.

SUGGESTIONS FOR FURTHER READING

In the Bible   Genesis 17, Psalm 103, Mark 10

A Book   *Children of Promise*, by G. Bromiley (T. & T. Clark)
             Theology in Reconciliation, by T. F. Torrance (chaps. 9 & 10) (SCM)
             I Believe in the Holy Spirit, by Michael Green (chaps. 6–9) (Hodder & Stoughton)

CHAPTER NINETEEN

Communion

Fellowship with God in the Spirit means daily prayer and Bible reading

Here we do not refer only to the sacrament of Holy Communion. The apostles were baptized in the Spirit of Pentecost, but from then on were 'filled with the Spirit'. Paul exhorts his readers to 'walk in the Spirit' and 'keep on being filled with the Spirit' (Ephesians 5:18).

Communion with Christ in the Spirit should be the foundation of the believer's DAILY LIFE. However, this communion with God in Christ is not an easy or cheap thing. Its basis, day by day, is the cross of Christ – his broken body and shed blood. That was the infinite cost of our daily fellowship with the Lord. So the Lord tells us to take up our cross daily and follow him. There is a daily need to ask the Lord to 'forgive us our trespasses and deliver us from evil', and that forgiveness and deliverance are based on the sufferings of the same Lord with whom we have communion.

The believer's communion with God is like a dialogue, that is, it is a relationship of hearing his Word and of speaking to him. So daily prayer and Bible reading are essential for the continuing communion. This is because we do not yet see our Lord 'face to face'. As with all aspects of our salvation, our fellowship with God, although begun in reality now, will only be brought to completion on the day of the Lord Jesus.

Although communion with God involves our feelings, particularly a feeling of love, it is not basically a relationship of feeling, but of knowledge, for faith is knowledge of the Unseen given us by the Holy Spirit. In human relationships of love, feelings come and go depending on circumstances. If the love is genuine (say between parent and child, husband and

wife), the love and knowledge of one another do not vary
with the feelings, but grow deeper with the passing of time. It
is the same in the believer's relationship with Jesus.

This daily Christian communion with man and God is
described in 1 John 1:7: 'If we walk in the light as he is in the
light, we have fellowship with one another and the blood of
Jesus his Son cleanses us from all sin.'

Holy Communion illustrates and seals this. Christ is really present in the sacrament, we receive him by faith

The sacrament which illustrates our communion with the
Lord, and not only illustrates it but seals it in our being, is the
sacrament of Holy Communion. It is a graphic reminder that
our fellowship with him depends on his body that was broken
for us and his blood that was shed for us. We do it in remembrance of him. The word 'remember' means more than just
'bring to mind'. The Lord's Supper is not a mere memorial, it
is a communion or participation with Christ in his death (1
Corinthians 10:16). Merely to remember the death of Christ
we would only need to look at the broken bread and poured
wine. But we do more, we eat the bread, and drink the wine,
proclaiming publicly to ourselves and our fellow believers
that we take him into our being. We eat the one loaf and
drink the cup together with the congregation of God's people,
demonstrating that even though we are many and varied,
still we are one body in the Spirit of Christ (1 Corinthians
10:17).

Through the Holy Spirit we 'feed on him in our hearts by
faith' (*Anglican Book of Common Prayer*). Continuing communion with Christ in his death and resurrection is graphically spoken of by Christ in John 6:53–54: 'Unless you
eat the flesh of the Son of Man and drink his blood, you have
no life in you; he who eats my flesh and drinks my blood has
eternal life, and I will raise him up at the last day.'

Unfortunately there has been much dispute as to the

nature of the feeding on Christ in Holy Communion. The traditional mediaeval belief was that the bread substantially changed into the body of Christ ('Transubstantiation'). That is to to say, although the bread still *appeared* like bread, there had been a change in its substance so that it really was the body of Christ. At the Reformation, the Lutherans rejected this and spoke of the substance of Christ's body being united to the bread, the bread itself remaining unchanged. This is called 'Consubstantiation'. Both these views involve confusing and unbiblical philosophical distinctions and definitions.

Some disciples took great offence at Jesus' words about eating his flesh and drinking his blood. His answer to them is interesting. He says 'Do you take offence at this? ... It is the Spirit that gives life, the flesh is of no avail; the words that I have spoken to you are Spirit and life' (John 6:61–63). Our feeding on Christ's flesh and blood is not physical but spiritual. The bread and the wine undergo no substantial change or substantial union with the body and blood of Christ, but the Holy Spirit uses the sacrament of Holy Communion to seal our daily spiritual union with Christ in faith. Christ is indeed really present in the sacrament, as he is in his Word, and we 'feed on him in our hearts by faith'. This is the Reformed doctrine of the Lord's Supper. In Holy Communion Christ is given to our hearts (not stomachs) by the Holy Spirit through faith.

The Lord's Supper should be celebrated often, and should be open to baptized children

Because Holy Communion is a reminder and seal of our daily communion with Christ it should be celebrated frequently. The Church of Scotland, in its history and in its General Assembly resolutions, has accepted this. The reason for not celebrating more frequently is not so much theological as practical. Presbyterians make such a big thing of it that it is very difficult to celebrate communion frequently. Perhaps if we did not make such a big thing of it, it would be able to have a larger place in our lives.

However, we do not want to fall into sacramentalism, where we base our whole communion with Christ on the sacrament. Our feeding on Christ is based even more on the reception of his Word. 'Man shall not live by bread alone, but by every word that proceeds from the mouth of God.' Communion with the Lord in the Spirit comes primarily from reading, hearing and preaching the Word of Go. the Bible, with faithful prayer. Without that the service of Holy Communion becomes superstition.

There is no good theological reason why children should not participate in the service of Holy Communion. God's grace is prior to our understanding, faith and repentance. The sacraments can even be described as 'converting ordinances' – though this does not of course mean that adults should come casually to the Lord's Table (1 Corinthians 11:28). Where there is an openness to the things of the Spirit of God, i.e. in a genuinely Christian home, then the Holy Spirit can work even in children. His work in children does not depend on a *mental* understanding. Christ's blessing of the little children was a *real* blessing, not just words. There is no reason why children who have been baptized should not receive Holy Communion as soon as they are physically able. If they received the sacramental sign and seal of entrance into the Kingdom, why should they be denied the sacramental sign and seal of continuing citizenship of the Kingdom?

Communion, sacrament of the Kingdom

The Lord's Supper, as a sacrament of the Kingdom, is not a gloomy feast. If it is solemn, it is only because it looks back to the cross, and we remember the cost of atonement. Yet even the cross is set in a context of joy. Jesus, for the joy set before him, endured the cross. So one of our hymns has the line, 'Sweet the wood and sweet the iron, and thy load how sweet is he'.

Communion

Moreover, the Supper looks forward to the great Supper of the Lord, when people from all over the world, and every age, sit at table in the Kingdom of God. It is the sacrament of the risen Christ. The word 'memorial' means more in Hebrew and Greek than in English! It means not just to remember events in the past, but to recall an action whose effect is present, so that by the Spirit not only are we taken back to the biblical drama of salvation, but Christ is with us now. And not only is Christ with us now, but we are taken up into heaven with him. We are always in a sense in heaven, as Christians (Colossians 3:1–4), but especially so at the Lord's Table.

Sometimes Christians are troubled by the warning in 1 Corinthians 11:27–29. That was written to people who had abused the Lord's Table as an excuse for getting drunk. We should pause indeed to examine ourselves. But the examination is not to see whether we are free from sin (who is?) but to recall that Christ died for sinners (1 Corinthians 11:29), and that in baptism we died with him (Romans 6:4). In the parable of the wedding feast, Jesus also warned us not to attempt to feast in God's kingdom without the right clothes – but clothes in Scripture are a symbol for the garment of holiness provided by God himself (e.g. Zechariah 3), and the poor invited by the King are also clothed by him.

The sacrament of communion holds out the Gospel to us. It offers Christ and all his blessings. And sometimes in God's wisdom it is the occasion of special signs of the Kingdom: healing and reconciliation.

SUGGESTIONS FOR FURTHER READING

In the Bible   Exodus 13, Psalm 105, 1 Corinthians 11

A Book   *In Remembrance of Me,* by David Cairns (Geoffrey Bles)
Table and Tradition, by Alasdair Heron (Handsel Press)

The Life of Faith

The Mystery of the Lord's Supper, by Robert Bruce
(James Clarke)
*Eucharist and Eschatology, by Geoffrey Wainwright
(Epworth Press)

CHAPTER TWENTY

Full Salvation

Salvation is complete in Christ

A number of Christian teachings down the ages in both Roman Catholic and Protestant churches have split salvation into distinct phases in the life of man. So, for example, a man may be taught that first he must be justified by having righteousness imputed to him, later sanctified by having righteousness imparted to him, and still later baptized in the Holy Spirit. The mistaken doctrine of grace already referred to is largely responsible for this. So in many 'Holiness' and 'Pentecostal' groups today a man may be uncertain as to where he actually is. Has he been justified but not yet sanctified, or maybe not yet baptized in the Spirit? Has he received Jesus as Saviour but not yet as Lord? All this leads to unnecessary introspection and confusion on the part of the believer, and is the cause of many leaving the Christian fold.

To receive Christ and have communion with him in the Spirit by faith, is to receive and have communion with the whole Christ. When we die and rise with him in baptism (Romans 6:3–4), leaving our pride and rebellion behind, and putting on his humility and obedience, Christ clothed with the full Gospel becomes ours. The fullness of the blessings of the Gospel must be understood in terms of the full exposition of Christ's threefold office as Priest, Prophet and King, giving us peace with God, sanctification (holiness), and deliverance from the powers of evil. He is our wisdom, our righteousness, our sanctification, our redemption (1 Corinthians 1:30).

Our salvation will only be complete on the day of the Lord Jesus when we fully enter into our inheritance. Then we shall see him 'face to face', having been delivered from even the presence of evil and temptation, and having been 'made like him'. So although the New Testament speaks of us as already having been saved, and continuing to be saved, it also tells us that 'we wait for the hope of righteousness' (Galatians 5:5). We in this world have the 'first fruits of the Spirit', so that even though we are children of God by adoption already, we still 'wait for adoption as sons, the redemption of our bodies'. In 'this hope we were saved' and so 'we wait for it with patience' (Romans 8:23–25). Until that day we are 'sealed with the promised Holy Spirit which is the guarantee of our inheritance until we acquire possession of it, to the praise of his glory' (Ephesians 1:13–14).

Justification, sanctification and deliverance, the first fruits of the Spirit, are past, present and future

Before the day of the Lord Jesus, we know the first fruits of the Spirit in our lives, namely justification, deliverance and sanctification.

(1) **Justification** 'Since we are justified by faith we have peace with God through our Lord Jesus Christ' (Romans 5:1). We noted in chapter 7 that one of the three main consequences of man's rebellion and pride was his separation from God. Through the sacrifice of Christ we are 'put right with God' (the phrase the *Good News Bible* rightly uses to interpret justification). The enmity between ourselves and God is taken away through Jesus' passive acceptance of the judgement of God upon our sin. As our living High Priest he restores us to fellowship with God, and so we are 'justified by his blood'.

Justification is a legal term taken from the law courts. To be justified is to be declared righteous and acquitted. The wonder of the Gospel is that through the death of Christ, God justifies the ungodly. He declares us righteous, not counting our sins against us. In other words, he forgives us all our sin, cancelling our guilt. In Romans 4:5–8 Paul's synonyms for 'justify' are 'reckon righteousness', 'remit sin', 'cover sins', 'not reckon sin' and 'forgive'.

Full Salvation

Justification means to 'put in the right'. So if a prisoner is found to be not guilty, he is put in the right relationship with the law by being set free. Justification in the Christian sense means not only being counted righteous but also being put in the right relationship with the Judge of all the earth. So justification means as well as being reckoned righteous, also being forgiven and reconciled to God. The terms 'justification' and 'reconciliation' are used interchangeably in Romans 5:9–12. Justification *is* reconciliation.

This right relationship with God is as child to father. God adopts us into his family and we call him 'Abba, Father'. On the basis of justification then, we approach God in prayer in the name of Jesus with the confidence that a little child has towards his father.

Our obedience to God is not the slavish obedience to written law, but the loving obedience of God's children to our heavenly Father. This is all possible because we are justified by faith, not by works of the law.

(2) **Sanctification** The second consequence of man's rebellion and pride, as we saw, is the spoiling of his nature, so that he becomes sinful. When the Son of God, the eternal prophetic 'Word of God', became flesh, he cleansed our human nature. He stretched out his divine hand and touched us in our worst place, namely our flesh of sin and death. Dying as representative man, standing in for humanity, he sanctified fallen man in his person.

In union with Christ, the Christian is sanctified and made holy in his inmost being. The love of God is put in his heart and so he begins to love God and his neighbour in holiness. He becomes a 'partaker of the divine nature' (2 Peter 1:4) and the image of God is refashioned within him.

The axe is laid at the root of the tree of sin, so that the whole tree begins to die. A new seed of love has been planted in him which grows and bears the fruit of the Spirit in his life, showing itself in good works.

The dying of the old tree of the flesh and the growing of the new tree of the Spirit continues throughout his life. The flesh

167

and the Spirit fight against each other (Galatians 5:16–17), so the believer must cultivate in his life the things of the Spirit and not the things of the flesh. 'For he who sows to his own flesh will from the flesh reap a harvest of death; but he who sows to the Spirit will from the Spirit reap eternal life' (Galatians 6:8).

The eternal purpose of God is that we 'be conformed to the image of his Son' (Romans 8:29). Our sanctification will be complete on the last day, for 'when he appears we shall be like him, for we shall see him as he is' (1 John 3:2). The pure in heart shall see God.

(3) **Deliverance from evil** 'He whom the Son sets free will be free indeed' (John 8:36). A consequence of man's rebellion and pride was his bondage to the forces of evil, particularly the accusing power of the devil. Christ, by deliberately setting himself to go to Jerusalem and die in our place as our substitute, set us free from the accusing power of the devil, bearing our sin in his body. Satan has no more power over those who are in Christ either to accuse them or to possess them. A Christian cannot be demon-possessed. God 'has delivered us from the dominion of darkness and transferred us to the kingdom of his beloved Son' (Colossians 1:13). We belong to Christ, to whom all power has been given because of his death. 'For to this end Christ died and lived again, that he might be Lord both of the dead and the living' (Romans 14:9).

In union with him we share his kingly power so that we are able to live as free men. 'You shall receive power when the Holy Spirit is come upon you' (Acts 1:8). This sets us free from all that binds us, so that the Christian should no longer be a slave to sin or have a dread of death. To continue to live in sin is a contradiction of the very purpose of the Gospel. 'The reason the Son of God appeared was to destroy the works of the devil, [so that] no one born of God practises sin' (1 John 3:8–9). We are set free from sin and set free to do good works, the works of faith.

However, since we only have the 'first fruits' of the Spirit,

Full Salvation

the presence of evil is still with us. Satan has no power over us, but he is able to tempt us. Sin no longer holds us in bondage, but we are not so free yet that we do not genuinely need to say regularly, 'Forgive us our trespasses and deliver us from evil'. Our deliverance, though real, is not yet complete.

The Spirit sets the Church apart for God and for the world, and the Church receives gifts from God for this purpose

So far in this chapter we have spoken of the work of the Spirit in us largely for *our* benefit. But the Spirit is given us that we might be for *God*, and for the *world*. This corresponds to the nature of wisdom as knowledge of God, nature and ourselves. And the Spirit is the Spirit of wisdom and of a sound mind.

(a) The Holy Spirit sets us apart *for God*. Our ministry of prayer is towards God (who sees in secret), whether praise, confession, thanksgiving, intercession or silent adoration. Some Christians receive the gift of tongues, which can deepen prayer life and give particular power to intercession, especially in situations of human despair and weakness. The gift can however be abused to encourage pride and laziness.

(b) The Spirit sets us apart *for one another*. We bear one another's burdens (Galatians 6:1). By this men know that we belong to Christ, that we love one another. Whoever is great in the Kingdom is the servant of his brothers and sisters. He shows the fruit of the Spirit (Galatians 5:22–26).

(c) The Spirit sets us apart *for the world*. 'Do good to all [but especially those of the household of faith].' As the Father sent Christ into the world, so Christ sends us. We go as his ambassadors (2 Corinthians 5:20), with his Spirit. The Church is the new Israel, a light for the world.

Through Baptism into Christ by the Spirit we share in the anointing of Christ to be Priest, Prophet and King. The whole Church is called to a priestly ministry, to confess the sins of mankind and to intercede for the world and its rulers; to a prophetic ministry – sharing in the world's situation and sorrow to preach the Gospel; to a kingly ministry, rebuking injustice, serving the poor, caring for those who are sheep without a shepherd that they may recognize the one good Shepherd.

To empower us for this varied service, God the Trinity gives gifts to the Church. There are three lists of these in the New Testament, and although different Greek words are used it is impossible to classify them neatly. We can, however, distinguish those gifts which all Christians should in principle be ready to receive and develop (in Romans 12:3–8 and 1 Corinthians 12:28–31 – these are not complete lists!), and those gifts which lead to certain people being set apart for leadership (in Ephesians 4:11–12: apostles, prophets, evangelists, pastors and teachers). The Reformed churches in particular tend to ordain men simply to 'the ministry' and allow gifts to be developed within that. But it should never be forgotten that *the ministry* is first that of Christ, and second, that of the whole people of God.

Healing. Full salvation lies in the future

The Spirit is a pledge of what is to come. Although the gift of healing, for example, may be given, it is a sign of God's love and power, not the complete answer. Not all are healed. It is important to present Christ in the context of what Koyama calls 'invitation theology', not 'answer theology'. He is the Truth, not the answer.

The two concepts which shed light on healing, and on the whole life of faith, are the active and the passive obedience of Christ. In his lifetime he waged war on disease and demons. In his death he bowed himself under the (temporary) power of evil in obedience to the mystery of his Father's will. So with us. Following the *active* obedience of Christ, we too wage war on sickness. We approve of medicine, and set it in the context of prayer whenever possible (James 5:13–16). We rejoice in special examples of divine healing. But we are

170

called also to follow the *passive* obedience of Christ, and to offer our suffering to God, like Paul, as a participation in the passion of Christ (Colossians 1:24).

We live and work by grace alone. The Church has not fulfilled her task. Her record is tarnished. She has lurched from one fault to another. In teaching dominion over nature, we have failed to teach responsibility towards nature. In stressing individual sin, we have failed to recognize social and structural sin. In meeting the needs of man's body, we have failed to meet the needs of his spirit – or vice versa. Lord, forgive us.

Full salvation lies in the future. The Church is on the road, travelling with Christ in the Spirit. We know in part. Salvation is complete in Christ, but only partially complete in us. 'This one thing I do,' testified Paul, 'forgetting what lies behind and straining forward to what lies ahead, I press on towards the goal for the prize of the upward call of God in Christ' (Philippians 3:13–14).

SUGGESTIONS FOR FURTHER READING

In the Bible   Ezekiel 47, Psalm 138, Revelation 1

A Book   *Calvin's Doctrine of the Christian Life*, by Ronald Wallace (Oliver & Boyd)
The Service of God, by C. E. D. Cranfield (Epworth Press)
Theology of Joy, by J. Moltmann (SCM)
The Open Secret, by Lesslie Newbigin (SPCK)